OPEN HANDS
WILLING HEART

VIVIAN MABUNI

OPEN HANDS
WILLING HEART

Discover the Joy of Saying Yes to God

WATERBROOK

Open Hands, Willing Heart

All Scripture quotations, unless otherwise indicated, are taken from the New American Standard Bible®. Copyright © 1960, 1962, 1963, 1968, 1971, 1972, 1973, 1975, 1977, 1995 by the Lockman Foundation. Used by permission. (www.Lockman.org). Scripture quotations marked (ESV) are taken from Holy Bible, English Standard Version, ESV® Text Edition® (2016), copyright © 2001 by Crossway Bibles, a publishing ministry of Good News Publishers. All rights reserved.

Trade Paperback ISBN 978-0-7352-9173-7
eBook ISBN 978-0-7352-9174-4

Copyright © 2019 by Vivian Mabuni

Cover design by Kristopher K. Orr; cover image by Shutterstock
Author photograph by Kenny Wong

Author is represented by Alive Literary Agency, 7680 Goddard Street, Suite 200, Colorado Springs, Colorado 80920, www.aliveliterary.com.

Published in the United States by WaterBrook, an imprint of the Crown Publishing Group, a division of Penguin Random House LLC, New York.

WaterBrook® and its deer colophon are registered trademarks of Penguin Random House LLC.

Library of Congress Cataloging-in-Publication Data
Names: Mabuni, Vivian, author.
Title: Open hands, willing heart : discover the joy of saying yes to God / Vivian Mabuni.
Description: First Edition. | Colorado Springs : WaterBrook, 2019. | Includes bibliographical references.
Identifiers: LCCN 2018040961 | ISBN 9780735291737 (pbk.) | ISBN 9780735291744 (electronic)
Subjects: LCSH: Christian women—Religious life.
Classification: LCC BV4527 .M198 2019 | DDC 248.8/43—dc23
LC record available at https://lccn.loc.gov/2018040961

Printed in the United States of America
2019—First Edition

10 9 8 7 6 5 4 3 2 1

Special Sales
Most WaterBrook books are available at special quantity discounts when purchased in bulk by corporations, organizations, and special-interest groups. Custom imprinting or excerpting can also be done to fit special needs. For information, please email specialmarketscms@penguinrandomhouse.com or call 1-800-603-7051.

Dedicated with love to Julia,
my favorite daughter, truly the world's best.
And to my amazing nieces, Cheyenne, Whitney,
Lexi, Angel, and Lauren.

May you live with intention and abandon to our King. May
you walk in joy and freedom. May your lives shine brightly
as you display God's glory through every part of your story.

The future is full of hope because of women like you.

In memory of Danielle Montiel.

You lived your time on earth with open hands and a willing
heart. Your prayer posture has become my own. I am
confident Jesus greeted you with the hugest embrace and
a hearty "Well done!" Can't wait to see you again.

A life well lived is a life surrendered.

Contents

Foreword

The subject of surrender is familiar to me. Sometimes I think it may be the only thing I've gotten right in my life. I've committed myself to say yes to God's leading, and He's moved in incredible ways. So many times I've said yes when it didn't make sense, and only years later did His plan become clear to me. Over and over He's used my yes to build amazing stories like IF:Gathering, which is where I got to meet Vivian.

Vivian is a yes kind of girl too, which is why her life is full of miracles, both in her family and in the lives of the many who count her as a spiritual mother. She even walked with open hands through the intense suffering of cancer. She says yes when she can't see the path ahead, and God shows up every time.

In college I was discipled through a ministry called Cru, and in many ways I can thank the leaders of that organization for my yes kind of faith. I'm grateful for how they taught me to love discipleship and live it as the primary goal of my life.

Cru is also where Vivian has spent her life saying yes. Every time I see her vibrant smile, I also see a string of younger women whose lives she's pouring herself into. And isn't that one of the best reasons to say yes? To invest ourselves in the lives of a few people who will love God more because we were here? That's something Vivian has mastered and cares about deeply.

Our choice to say yes is rarely easy, but it's our sacrifice that gives meaning to our surrender. Most of my yeses have cost me in different ways, but all of them have been worth it: adopting, carrying casseroles across the street for neighbors who just moved in, teaching the Bible to one or a thousand, having hard conversations, and saying yes in all the unseen circumstances of everyday life. It's worth it. All of it is worth it. When we get to heaven, we'll celebrate every yes we said and the ways God used our short lives for His eternal purposes.

We have much to learn from Vivian through the pages of this book. And one day when we all get to heaven, I'll be right there to hug and thank this beautiful woman for her willingness to say yes to running this race beside me and to sharing God with others in ways that have shaped eternity.

—Jennie Allen, founder and visionary, IF:Gathering

PART 1

A WILLING HEART

A Posture of the Heart

No one can sum up all God is able to accomplish through one solitary life, wholly yielded, adjusted, and obedient to Him.

—D. L. MOODY

The hot sun beat down relentlessly on sixteen-year-old Florence. Her stomach rumbled as she brushed sweat from her brow. As the firstborn of her siblings, she shouldered many household responsibilities, including finding adequate places for the family's cows to graze. Like many other Rwandans in the 1960s, Florence's parents had fled their homeland and crossed into neighboring Uganda as refugees fleeing political upheaval and bloodshed. Florence, born in Uganda, gave her life to Christ as a fifteen-year-old. She remembers praying and setting in her heart a memorial.

"You never, ever forget about this decision. It is a special thing you have done."

On this particular day while tending the cows, Florence unsuc-cessfully searched for fruit among the bushes. Barefoot, hungry, thirsty, and hot, Florence longed for more. As she looked around at her environment and considered the projected path for girls her age, she knew unless something changed, her current circumstances would keep her walking long distances to fetch water and lacking opportu-nity to do what she most desired.

Florence recalls with both vividness and fondness the exact area near the rocks and stones where God led her. The rock she stood on became another memorial, the place she prayed her first prayer of deep commitment and surrender. As the first believer in her family, and brand-new in her faith, she didn't know the exact mechanics of how to pray. She knew only to bring to God her deepest heart desire. With honesty and sincerity she prayed, "Jesus, if You are really real, would You give me education?" Added to this heartfelt prayer, she promised, "If You give me education, I will commit to serve You forever and tell everyone how great You are."

Florence's simple prayer of surrender released control of her life to her heavenly Father. Her hands now opened to have the Lord take and give as He saw fit.

Land of a Thousand Hills

A few years ago on a trip to Rwanda, I had the joy of hearing and see-ing how God answered Florence's prayer.

Rwanda. A vibrant land filled with vibrant people who are resil-ient and remarkable. The country continues to make tremendous strides after the horrific genocide that took place in 1994, when government officials carried out plans for the mass extermination of an entire ethnic people group and any sympathizers. Between April and July more than eight hundred thousand men, women, and children died from the mass slaughter over the course of ninety days. In addition to the torturous deaths, an estimated five hundred thousand women were raped and intentionally infected with HIV. The aftermath of the genocide left four hundred thousand orphans. The brutality, cruelty, and horror remain unfathomable. But I saw with my own eyes how out of death and what seemed irreparable, God brought new life.

I was privileged to be part of a team of twenty-two women who traveled to Rwanda to experience firsthand the beautiful ministry God is doing in and through the women there. The trip rose out of a mutually beneficial partnership between Africa New Life ministry (ANL) in Rwanda and IF:Gathering, a worldwide Christian movement founded by my friend Jennie Allen with a mission to gather, equip, and unleash women to live out God's calling for their lives.

I have had the honor of teaching and equipping leaders through IF and have forged relationships with incredible women who, like Jennie, love God fiercely. For that trip in the summer of 2017, God put together a team composed of women from different parts of the country, with different stories, bringing different gifts, living in different stages of life, and experiencing different life circumstances. God used our differences to meet each situation we encountered. We lived out the truth of how we are better together. God taught me about faith, dedication, trust, and dependence through these new sisters when our feet hit the red soil of Rwanda.

Our first day in Rwanda, we toured the ANL ministry center. Still new to each other and learning names, while adjusting to the elevation and time change, our team assembled to hear about the early days of the ministry from one of the founders, Florence Mugisha.

Florence paced slowly back and forth before us as she recounted her story, including her teenage prayer of surrender. Eight years after Florence began a relationship with Jesus, she began attending a Bible college in Uganda. There she met her future husband, Charles. Both Rwandans, Florence and Charles longed to return home to minister to the orphan children left behind after the genocide. After they married, they served at a church in Uganda where they received no monthly paycheck. They welcomed their first son, Isaac, and entered a time of what Florence described as "crazy faith." Their refrigerator sat empty when an unexpected gift of one hundred euros arrived from a donor in England. An opportunity to sponsor nine Rwandan children opened up around the same time. Charles asked Florence if they could give the money they received to the children so they could attend school.

Charles didn't push. Florence struggled. They had no food. They needed milk. But something she'd once heard played in her mind: "Small, painful seeds give rise to huge ministries." She wondered, *Could this be the seed?* She explained to us, "It wasn't exciting, but it was an opportunity, and I knew I needed to say yes."

In November 2000 God opened doors for their small family to move to Portland, Oregon, to study at Multnomah University. Before they moved to America, they sold or gave away their belongings in Uganda, including all their wedding presents. They lived in the basement of a home of a host family in exchange for babysitting and taking care of the laundry and housework. Everything felt strange and unfamiliar. Florence didn't know anyone, her family lived thousands of miles away, and she felt lonely and out of place. But through her willingness to sacrifice and do whatever God asked, her relationship with Him deepened.

Florence dreamed of someday owning a house in Rwanda, a small two-bedroom home for her little family that they would not have to rent. To her surprise the host family paid her when she babysat. Florence saved up every penny. As much as she wanted to go shopping at the fancy malls, she refrained, saving every dollar for her future home. Over time she saved $1,000.

Two years later Charles and Florence traveled back to Rwanda to determine next steps for the ministry God had placed on their hearts. Seeing firsthand the orphans, the widows, the refugees, and the hurting families broke their hearts. The needs they saw before them compelled them to look into how they could formally begin to help. They felt led to rent a small home to start a preschool as a springboard for future ministry. Charles learned that in order to register a ministry to receive wire transfers and funds, they needed to set up a bank account.

Charles turned to Florence. "Can we use your money?"

Florence did see the money as hers. She had been the one to work the long hours watching the hosts' children. She had been the one to wash and fold all the laundry. Of the money she had earned, she hadn't spent a penny on herself. She had sacrificed to save for her dream. Now Charles had the audacity (or perhaps the faith?) to ask Florence for the money to open the bank account and rent the small home.

Charles didn't push. Florence wrestled. It didn't seem fair. But more than to own her own home, the desire of Florence's heart was to please God and glorify Him. Once again she opened her hands, and in faith she gave what she had to the Lord and to Charles.

Hearing Florence share her story, I couldn't hold back tears. We were sitting in the Dream Center, which grew out of the seed money she'd relinquished to the Lord. Her example of living with open hands and a willing heart touched tens of thousands of lives. I marveled thinking about the more than nine thousand children now sponsored by their organization. Florence continued to be burdened for the women in Rwanda, so she also began a ministry to help at-risk women learn vocational skills. Our team worshipped with the ninety women enrolled in the year-long sewing and beauty-school program. Another ministry sponsored by ANL is the Africa College of Theology. The 576 seminary students enrolled come from all over Rwanda and neighboring countries. The seminary trains and equips pastors and recently added book-printing facilities. Multnomah University donated twenty thousand books to the seminary library, now one of the largest libraries in Rwanda. Later our group toured the Dream Medical Center and visited the schools and churches established in other cities across the country. Over and over Florence and her family had sacrificed and followed God's leading, and He had shown Himself faithful.

Open-Handed Living

As women after God's heart, you and I desire to please God and be aligned with His will. We want to be used by Him and experience the peace and fulfillment He wants for us. It's all too easy, though, to fall into living mechanically, with a rule-based approach to the Christian life, or to get too focused on what we want when we want it. When life isn't unfolding the way we thought it would, we wonder if we're on track with who He would have us be and what He would have us do. We long for more fulfillment, contentment, and meaning, but above all we want to see our lives from His perspective and experience more of Him.

The path to saying yes to whatever God asks often feels scary, though, and the distractions of this world get in the way even when we want to be willing. But open-handed living is worth everything it asks of us because it makes our day-to-day lives more purposeful, powerful, and pleasing to God. When our hearts are surrendered to Him and aligned with His will, we draw closer to Him in a way that unleashes His grand purposes for our lives.

What I have learned over several decades of following Jesus is that the essence of surrender is in the posture of our hearts. It is the spirit of following Jesus with hands and hearts open, humbly letting go of whatever we tend to clutch and control as we seek His perspective in all things. When we are in this place of surrender, we give the Holy Spirit free rein to direct and sustain our journey and we realize that our lives are part of a much greater story: God's story of hope and restoration in the lives of individuals, families, communities, churches, and society.

Not long before his death, Henri Nouwen wrote in *Sabbatical Journeys* about some friends who were trapeze artists. They shared with Nouwen about the special relationship between flyer and catcher on the trapeze. The flyer lets go, and the catcher catches. As the flyer swings high above the crowd on the trapeze, the moment comes when she must let go. She arcs out into the air, where her sole job is to remain as still as possible as she opens her hands and waits for the strong hands of the catcher to pluck her to safety. One of the trapeze artists told Nouwen, "The flyer must never try to catch the catcher." The catcher will catch the flyer, but she must wait in absolute trust. Similarly, open-handed living calls us to let go in the midst of risk and uncertainty, aligning our heart posture and choices with God's will for our lives.

My first big surrender came shortly after beginning a relationship with Jesus in high school. My dad went through a midlife crisis, which included a fancy sports car (woo-hoo!) followed by a perm (another story, another time) and then the news that we would be moving right before my senior year from Colorado to Hong Kong. Angry and confused, I unleashed my frustration and let God know exactly how I felt about the situation. But at the end of my tirade, I added a sincere "In my heart of hearts, I really want to know You and do Your will." In Hong Kong I gave God control of my life at a whole new level. I moved over and let Him have the driver's seat. He would be the Good Shepherd who would lead and provide—the center, the source, the focus. I would give Him first place in my life and let Him take me wherever He thought best.

I came to another crossroads as I graduated from college. Law school? Vocational Christian ministry? Serving God in an international setting seemed exciting and even glamorous to my twenty-something self. I wasn't afraid to minister overseas, but I did wrestle with what I considered my worst-case scenario: driving an ugly, out-dated car and living in complete isolation and obscurity doing boring, mundane work day in and day out. Nevertheless, I remember praying a tearful but sincere prayer of surrender: "God, I will go wherever You want me to go—even if You ask me to drive one of those old station wagons with fake wood paneling on the outside and to work and live all alone. Even then I will choose to follow You."

Each time I've placed my heart, life, plans, hopes, and dreams into the hands of my loving, good, strong, faithful, able, and all-knowing God, it has simultaneously been easier and harder. Looking back, I see that His faithfulness has proved to be unwavering, so making the choice to trust Him seems the most reasonable option. Yet what God asks me to trust Him with sometimes requires more of me as my life progresses and grows more complicated. I find there is more at stake.

When faced with my own cancer diagnosis a few years ago, I prayed another surrender prayer. Every morning I awakened in the dark with my mind racing, wondering if the diagnosis was a bad dream. As my mind cleared and the heavy reality set in, I would make my way upstairs to my little nook where I poured out my fears to the God I have learned to trust. I wrestled with what seemed like reasonable, honorable desires of living to witness the major milestones in my three kids' lives. I wanted a front-row seat. The willingness to yield my plans and open my hands, even to let go of my very life, became a moment-by-moment choice.

Sometimes, though, I find myself trying to manipulate God; I want to control the outcome of my circumstances. I pray with directives: "This is how You need to answer, God, and this is how You need to fix this situation." But over the years I've come to realize that no two situations are alike and God will deliver in the way He sees fit. Each time He does it a little differently so that we learn to rely on *Him* rather than on a formula that worked in the past, a business model we read in a book, our personal gifts, or our previous experience.

Consider what this implies about how God works in your life. Take a moment and look at your left thumb. The combination of lines and swirls that make your thumbprint belongs to you alone. No one on this planet of 7.5 billion people shares the same print. That you are reading or listening to this book right now means you are still on special assignment. God crafts unique purposes for you, giving you the opportunity to participate as He unfolds His plans. Maybe you are struggling over important life scenarios: your marital status, your finances, your job, your children, your character defects, or your health. Perhaps an unhealthy relationship has taken center stage in your life and God is asking you to let go and turn the relationship over to Him. Perhaps God has given you clarity on an area of disobedience and is calling you to confess and turn from the sin. God may be calling you to live more purposefully, less busily, or less complacently. Maybe you are finally getting honest about your eating disorder, addiction, anxiety, or depression, and God is asking you to humble yourself and seek help from a trained professional. Perhaps His Spirit is encouraging you to forgive the person who hurt you, or He wants you to get out from under the weight of trying to please others and follow their will rather than His.

When I read Scripture, I am reminded of how God is the one who determines our boundaries and the exact places we should live (Acts 17:26). He makes no mistakes as He skillfully weaves us together in our mothers' wombs (Psalm 139:13). We are born into this world without control over our family of origin; we have no say in who our parents are, the number of siblings we grow up with, or our birth order. We have no control over our gender, ethnic makeup, cultural heritage, family history, socioeconomic class at birth, or gifts and wiring. But God has His reasons for forming us as He has. "We are his workmanship, created in Christ Jesus for good works, which God prepared beforehand, that we should walk in them" (Ephesians 2:10, ESV). We may not have the opportunity to see the direct outcome of our choices or live the life we always dreamed of, but God maps out for us a way to walk in freedom from our expectations of how we think life should unfold, even when our circumstances don't make sense to us. He continually asks us to let go and trust that He will catch us. He invites us to relinquish control in the midst of the unknown, the unanswered questions, the bewildering circumstances, and the sense of being overwhelmed. In this place of surrender, we deepen our intimacy with Him. Our challenge is to relinquish what hinders us from seeking and following His will, wherever it may take us.

A Story of Surrender

One character in the Bible I find both fascinating and inspiring is the orphan Hadassah, whose name is Hebrew for "myrtle." A myrtle is an evergreen shrub or tree with fragrant white flowers. While we are not given much information about Hadassah's childhood, an entire book in the Bible is written about her under her Persian name, Esther.

We will unpack Esther's story in the pages ahead (as well as stories from other folks in Scripture), but here's a brief summary. Esther was adopted and raised by her cousin Mordecai and grew up in Persia, now southwestern Iran, as part of the Jewish remnant that chose to remain in voluntary exile rather than return to their homeland. Her family was exiled in 586 BC when King Nebuchadnezzar destroyed Jerusalem. Forty-seven years later, under the rule of Cyrus the Great of

Persia, Jews were allowed to return to Palestine. Esther's story takes place fifty-six years after their return.

The king at that time, Xerxes, called Ahasuerus in some translations, had a wife who was beautiful but refused to do his bidding. This infuriated him, and after consulting with his advisers, he decided to banish Queen Vashti and replace her with someone more compliant. Xerxes sent out harem scouts to round up young virgin girls for his consideration. This was no volunteer beauty pageant. These young girls, including Esther, were wrenched from their families to become part of the king's collection. Esther pleased the king more than any of the other women, so Xerxes crowned her queen.

We find elsewhere in Scripture examples of God's people living in foreign lands and making God-honoring choices. Joseph was sold into Egyptian slavery yet remained faithful to God (Genesis 39). Daniel and his friends were swept up in the Babylonian exile and chose not to partake in the consumption of food unlawful to them. They refused idol worship and retained their devotion to God at all costs (Daniel 1–3). Though not explicitly stated in the text, it seems Esther's case was different. Her cousin Mordecai instructed her to hide her Jewish roots, and she did so. Esther chose to go along with the surrounding culture and disobeyed several commandments from the Mosaic law. She kept her identity a secret and relied on her outer beauty to keep the king's favor. She lived a life of comfort and privilege, with her foremost aim to please her husband, not her God.

Sometimes God uses a crisis to jolt us out of living for our own protection and comfort. In Esther's case her crisis came when King Xerxes sent forth a decree to annihilate all the Jews living within his kingdom. Esther was a Jewish exile, a woman, married to the king, with access to leaders who could determine the fate of her people's lives. However, Persian laws set in place to protect the king from assassination attempts made approaching him without being summoned punishable by death. Esther had a life-and-death decision to make.

We see the evidence of her surrendered heart when, after much fasting and prayer, she decided to approach the king unannounced and accept the outcome, good or bad. "If I perish, I perish," she declared (Esther 4:16). Esther recognized her unique role at this particular time in history and acknowledged that her life belonged entirely to God.

In this posture, with her hands open to the one true King, Esther yielded her will and allowed God to give or take as He saw fit. God's great purposes were unleashed as Esther let go of her one-dimensional, skin-deep existence. She rose up as a leader who wisely, shrewdly, boldly risked her life in behalf of her people. Through Esther the Jewish people were delivered; even people living in Persia became followers of her God (8:17). Esther's example revealed her dependence on the Lord and demonstrated how God works in mysterious ways to change the hearts of kings (Proverbs 21:1).

A Willing Heart

Having a willing heart like Esther's and Florence's requires that we pursue a relationship with God above all others. Following Jesus isn't so much a decision to live a particular lifestyle with stringent rules as it is a decision to live in relationship *with* Him and allow Him to lead, guide, provide, and sustain. In Florence's words, "Surrender. Let God be God."

Throughout the rest of this book, we will delve into what this might look like in our lives and what gets in the way. Sometimes having a willing heart means that we release our tight grip on what we think will give us security; our open hands then become conduits for God to bless and redirect resources as needed. Our willing hearts overcome apathy and let go of entitlement, refusing to settle for anything less than what God wants for us. Our willing hearts depend on God rather than on our limited resources. Our willing hearts learn the rhythms of restorative rest and avoid burnout. Our willing hearts extend forgiveness to others as we walk in the forgiveness we receive in Christ. Our willing hearts trust that God's timing is perfect and that the times when He tells us no or to wait are never haphazard or cruel. Our willing hearts serve by faith, often not knowing what will be the outcome of our sacrifices and choices. Our willing hearts move toward others with different backgrounds and experiences. Our willing hearts receive the spiritual nourishment that only Christ can provide. And our willing hearts walk by faith through the doors God opens and follow whatever path He lays out, even if it looks nothing like what we planned.

But where do we start to align ourselves more closely with God's will? How do we surrender our wills if they are at odds with God's? Believing that the center of God's will is the best place to be is one thing; living out that belief in our daily lives is another.

A few years ago, on a flight leaving my home airport in Southern California, I sat next to a man who kept looking out the window of the plane with more than usual interest. As we got acquainted, I learned that he piloted smaller planes as a hobby and often flew out of our airport. He shared with me how the runway identifying numbers need to be adjusted as the earth's magnetic poles gradually shift over time. The compass the airplanes use always points to magnetic north, but the numbers no longer accurately reflect the magnetic heading of the runways as the magnetic poles change position.

The same shifting is true of us. Our hearts need regular recalibration to stay in line with God's will. We become recalibrated as we lift our eyes off self and circumstances and turn our attention wholly to God. Letting go of whatever "trapeze" we might be holding on to requires trust. Not trust in ourselves; not trust in particular outcomes; but trust in the One who loves us and promises to catch us.

Yes, living with a willing heart can take us down painful roads. Sometimes our pain is the result of our poor choices. Other times the poor choices of others affect our lives. Sometimes no clear correlation exists, and we are confused and bewildered. While God may allow sickness, pain, and death for purposes we don't always understand, He never abandons us in our sorrow. He never lies or forgets or lashes out. He is not ego driven or insecure or power hungry. He is good. He is near. His love is tender and fierce.

I imagine God scanning the earth, spotting young Florence in the middle of western Uganda as she lifted up to heaven her surrendered heart, and smiling in delight, knowing the plans He had already laid out for her. God sees each of us as well, and He knows our hearts. Those whose hearts belong wholly to Him have His strong support.

As I looked across the grounds of the Dream Center and back at Florence that day, I kept thinking, *Look what happened when she opened her hands.*

 *Questions for Reflection and Discussion*

1. What part of Florence's story most challenges or inspires
    you?

2. Have you experienced a time when you were challenged
    to have "crazy faith"? If so, what did you learn from that
    experience?

3. Describe a time when God prompted you to give or let go of
    something you were reluctant to relinquish. If you were able
    to let go, what was the outcome?

4. How would you describe the posture of your heart at this
    time in your life? What are some things you clutch or try to
    control that might be preventing you from letting go of the
    "trapeze"?

5. Consider my statement "Each time I've placed my heart, life,
    plans, hopes, and dreams into the hands of my loving, good,
    strong, faithful, able, and all-knowing God, it has simultane-
    ously been easier and harder." In what ways has this been
    true for you?

6. Has God ever used a crisis to jolt you out of living for your own protection and comfort, as He did with Esther? If so, describe the experience and what you learned about yourself and God through it.

7. What similarities can you see between yourself and Esther? Discuss a time when you had to make a hard choice to follow God's plan for your life.

8. Is there an area of your life right now that feels at odds with God's will for you? If so, ask God to better align your heart posture with His purposes for you. Commit to reading and studying this book to learn how to live with open hands, fully surrendered to Him.

Esther

A Portrait of Surrender

Queen Esther's long, delicate fingers smoothed the satin fabric. The intricate embroidery and vibrant colors still evoked awe. Her pre-palace life never exposed her to such beautiful clothing, even during the most festive celebrations back home. It occurred to her that her everyday wear, carefully selected by the maidens who waited on her, would probably disappear into a room full of equally exquisite clothing and never be worn again. The quantity and quality of clothing matched her posh surroundings. Marble, gold, precious jewels, and exotic flowers filled her world as far as her deep-brown eyes could see.

But Esther missed her life in the province where she grew up, before she was rounded up by King Xerxes's harem scouts and eventually chosen to be queen. Back home she was known by her given name, Hadassah, and when she closed her eyes now, she could almost hear her friends calling, "Hadassah, Hadassah, hurry up and finish your chores so you can come down and play!" She missed the smell of the familiar foods from her childhood. She missed her friends and the simple lifestyle and predictable pace. Though at times she had struggled with not fitting in after losing both her parents, her tight-knit community rallied, and she knew they would always love, protect, and support her. She let out a deep sigh as she thought about her faraway friends and faraway life.

As she sat quietly in the shade, she continued to rub the edge of her sash between her thumb and forefinger. The motion helped soothe her racing heart as she anticipated King Xerxes returning home from war. His volatile temper and propensity to make rash decisions, especially when under the influence of alcohol and his nefarious advisers, kept everyone in the palace walking on eggshells.

Xerxes spent his days alternating between strategizing about expanding his influence and gathering the best the world had to offer. Every detail in the palace surroundings served to further his reputation of greatness. As his beautiful trophy wife, the new queen added to the king's collection of the finest of everything. The name he'd given Hadassah, Esther, was derived from the Persian word for "star." This underscored the expectations placed on her in her new role. She dutifully learned from Hegai, one of the king's eunuchs, and sought to attend to every detail of what the king liked and disliked.

Esther found great comfort in knowing that her cousin Mordecai, her only living blood relative, sat at the king's gate. Mordecai had raised her as his own daughter after her parents died, and because he wanted to know how she fared inside the palace, he became a regular at the gate. In fact, because he stayed close, he happened to overhear a plot to assassinate the king. He reported the information to Esther, and when an investigation confirmed the plans, the king had Mordecai's good deed recorded in his Book of the Chronicles.

The quiet moment evaporated as angry footsteps echoed down the marble hallway. Tension filled the air. One of the king's top advisers, Haman, stormed past with clenched fists and an ugly vein popping out along the temples of his red face and furrowed brow. Esther knew his rage was fueled by her cousin's refusal to bow and pay homage to Haman at the king's gate. Haman glared at the servant standing near the door and forcefully pushed him aside, knocking down a large hand-painted vase from the Far East. A thousand pieces of priceless porcelain scattered across the hallway. The irreparable shards lay motionless, the moment blanketed by thick silence. All the palace servants froze until Haman disappeared behind the immense double doors.

Though Haman filled a powerful and important position over all the nobles, he was an insecure little man. No amount of prominence or accolades quenched his lust for power and influence. As far as Haman was concerned, Mordecai the Jew was a threat. Haman's hatred ran deep.

Within a few days, word came that Haman had offered to pay 375 tons of his own silver to the kingdom treasury if Xerxes agreed to let him set in motion the murder of Mordecai and all the Jewish people living in the kingdom. With the king's approval and his signet ring sealing the decree, the plan became ironclad.

According to Persian law, not even the king himself could reverse the orders.

Confusion and anguish filled the hearts of the Jewish people as they learned of the impending slaughter. Mordecai responded with a public display of lament by donning sackcloth and ashes and wailing bitterly as he walked from the city to the king's gate. When Esther got wind of her cousin's condition, she sent clean garments with the king's eunuch Hathach. Mordecai refused the clothing and sent back a copy of the edict explaining the planned destruction of all the Jews. Years earlier Mordecai had instructed Esther to keep her Jewish identity a secret. Now he asked her to approach the king and plead for her people.

To protect the king and prevent possible assassination attempts, only the king's advisers were granted free access to Xerxes. All others, including his wife, could approach only if the king summoned them. The punishment for approaching the king without an invitation was death unless he showed favor by holding out his golden scepter.

Esther had not seen Xerxes in over a month. His unpredictable mood swings made her blood run cold. She was naturally terrified to approach. But Mordecai's words seared her heart. "If you keep silent at this time," he had said, "relief and deliverance will rise for the Jews from another place, but you and your father's house will perish. And who knows whether you have not come to the kingdom for such a time as this."

The families in the province Esther came from passed along to their children the history of God's deliverance throughout the generations. Esther remembered the stories of desperate times when her people humbled themselves and cried out for help. She ordered Mordecai to have all the Jews living in Xerxes's kingdom fast from food and water for three days and nights. Mordecai did as his young cousin directed. She would always hold the place of daughter in his heart. Esther and her maidens would also fast and pray.

Esther retired to her royal chamber and glanced around the room. A group of young maidens stood quietly in the shadows, anticipating all the queen's needs and wants. They lived to do her bidding. But in that moment the grand furnishings in her chamber lost their splendor for Esther. No single thing could replace a person's life. Esther had grown accustomed to living with external abundance, but comfort and security paled as she realized how meaning could not be found in acquisitions or appearances or position or power.

Esther knew she didn't own any of the extravagance surrounding her. She filled a role as queen, but everyone knew her position could change in a split second if the king had a bad day. Even her beauty, which opened doors and at times led to preferential treatment, would eventually fade. The only aspect of her life that truly belonged to her was the posture of her heart before her God.

Esther considered her choices. She knew that many of the decisions she had made since arriving in Xerxes's kingdom violated the Mosaic law of her people. As she sat by the window of her chambers, she surrendered both her shortcomings and her situation. An unexplainable peace flooded her from head to toe.

On the third morning her maidens meticulously dressed Esther in her royal robes. They marveled at the queen's serene disposition. But Esther knew deep down she would not approach the king's throne alone. Regardless of the outcome, she moved confidently under the direction of the One who knew her best and who acted with perfect faithfulness.

Esther stood calmly in the court, and the king allowed her to approach him. She invited the king and Haman for a private banquet, and Xerxes agreed. The conversation over dinner centered on the king's latest accomplishments and acquisitions—topics he liked to focus on. The finest wine flowed liberally, and Xerxes, with his heart merry, asked Esther what her request was, even offering up to half the kingdom should she desire.

Following her intuition, Esther, with the sweetest of smiles and a twinkle in her eye, simply requested that the two men join her for another feast. Haman's happiness over anticipating another evening of being wined and dined by the stunning queen dissolved when later he saw Mordecai at the palace gate, still refusing to bow to him. Haman became furious, and his wife suggested he build a tall gallows and have Mordecai killed and put on display the next day. This temporarily quelled his rage.

That night the king tossed and turned and woke with his mind racing. He called out to his servant to read the memorable deeds recorded in his Book of the Chronicles, hoping the servant's monotone voice would carry him back into slumber. The book happened to open to the pages that detailed the plan to assassinate the king and how Mordecai saved the day. The king asked if Mordecai had received any honor or distinction for his act of valor. The servant carefully scanned page after page of the large book. "Nothing has been done for him," he said.

The next day Haman came to talk to the king about having Mordecai hung. Before a word escaped his lips, the king asked, "What should be done to the man whom the king delights to honor?" Haman saw this as his moment. He wanted to experience life as royalty. He wanted to wear the king's robe, ride the king's royal horse, and be led into the public square where his status would be recognized. As he suggested these things to the king, a wide smile of agreement spread across Xerxes's face. Haman could not have been more stunned when the king said, "Hurry; take the robes and the horse, as you have said, and do so to Mordecai the Jew, who sits at the king's gate. Leave out nothing that you have mentioned."

Bitterly, Haman obeyed the king's orders, leading the king's horse with Mordecai mounted and adorned in the king's robe and declaring throughout the city square how the king shows honor to those in whom he delights.

Completely humiliated, Haman showed up late to Esther's second banquet. He noticed that the atmosphere was decidedly cooler. After dinner the king asked a second time what Esther wished for. This time she asked for her life and the lives of her people. When further questioned, the queen singled out Haman as the one who had initiated the plan to destroy her people. Furious, the king left to find officials to discipline Haman.

Terrified, Haman fell at Esther's feet, begging for his life. When the king returned and saw Haman lying over the queen on the couch, an enraged Xerxes accused Haman of assaulting the queen. Harbonah, one of the king's eunuchs, volunteered information about the gallows Haman had built for Mordecai. Without hesitation the king commanded that Haman be hung on the gallows. Haman's wails filled the palace as the servants dragged him away. Then the king gave Mordecai permission to amend the decree of death to the Jews, allowing the people to defend themselves against attack with the backing of the king's signet ring and signature.

Word spread far and wide at the thrilling news of deliverance, and the Jews celebrated with a feast and a holiday. As a result of the events that transpired, the Jews were saved and the nation of our Redeemer was preserved. One orphaned young woman, through her willingness to surrender her heart and life to her God, changed the course of history.[1]

2

A God Who Can Be Trusted

God is so vastly wonderful, so utterly and completely
delightful that He can, without anything other than
Himself, meet and overflow the deepest demands of our
total nature, mysterious and deep as that nature is.

—A. W. Tozer, *The Pursuit of God*

I think my water broke." My best friend from college, Pam, had flown
down from the San Francisco Bay Area for my baby shower, and afterward we went out to dinner. On the way home I felt warm liquid seep
out of my body. When I got out of the car, a small spot of blood stained
the seat. The excitement of the day's events turned to mild concern. At
our last Lamaze class two days earlier, the instructor had mentioned a
"bloody show" some women had at the beginning of labor. Maybe this
was it, but the baby wasn't due for three more weeks.

We walked up the stairs to our apartment, and I told my husband,
Darrin, what had happened. He put in a call to our doctor, but another

doctor on call told him, "Wait until the contractions are five minutes apart before you go to the hospital."

Even though I couldn't feel any notable contractions, Darrin called the hospital. They asked him what the doctor instructed and told him to follow doctor's orders and wait until the contractions were five minutes apart. Meanwhile I continued to bleed, waiting for contractions that never came.

We placed another call to the unhelpful doctor, who told us to wait some more. Another call to the hospital. The nurse must have heard the unease in Darrin's voice because she said, "Go ahead and bring her in, and we can take a look." By this point the blood flowed so heavily I was sitting on a rolled-up beach towel.

When we arrived at the hospital, they took one look at me and the beach towel and whisked me off to a room. Immediately nurses began running back and forth with clipboards and papers to sign. They strapped a heartbeat monitor around my abdomen. I could hear that the baby's heartbeat wasn't right; it was weak and faint. Tension filled the room.

Just the day before, at my thirty-seven-week checkup, everything had checked out fine, including the strong and steady sound of the baby's heartbeat. The doctor mentioned how pleased he was with how smoothly the pregnancy had gone. At the conclusion of the appointment, he told me that since I wasn't dilated yet, the baby wouldn't be coming anytime soon.

Now, as I heard the faint heartbeat, I started to panic. I looked up at the name tag of the nurse hovering over me. "Lynn," it said, and next to her name was a Christian fish symbol. I grabbed her arm.

"Excuse me, are you a Christian?"

"Oh, yes. And so is the nurse over there."

Through tears of fear and relief, I told her, "I'm a Christian too."

Lynn took my hand and said, "Don't worry. I will be praying for you and the baby all the way through."

Those were the last words I remember hearing as they wheeled me off to surgery. I couldn't stop shaking. I stared up at the fluorescent lighting, watching the hospital ceiling tiles go by overhead and thinking, *This isn't how I thought it was going to be.*

They put me under anesthesia for an emergency Cesarean section. I later learned that I had *abruptio placentae.* My placenta had started separating from my uterine wall. Thanks to modern medicine and a whole bunch of grace, I gave birth to a healthy son.

My doctor came to see me at the hospital the next day. "Angels must have been watching over you," he said. "Your placenta was one-third separated. Any more and it could have been fatal for the baby or for you." He mentioned the angels again as he left. Both Darrin and I knew without question that God was looking out for us. Lynn, the nurse, came by, and I found out she hadn't been scheduled to work the night before but came in at the last moment.

After the doctor left, we somehow managed to move me from the bed into a wheelchair. Darrin carefully pushed me, with various tubes and IV pole in tow, down the hallway to meet our son in the neonatal intensive care unit. A nurse had taken a Polaroid picture of our son and taped it to the side of my bed so I could see it when I came out of surgery. I tried matching the photo to the babies in the room. In the corner I spied a baby with a head full of jet-black hair. As we wheeled closer, I saw a tube stuck into his nose for feeding; then I noticed his tiny feet bandaged from multiple pricks for blood work. I'd been unconscious for the birth. How could I be sure this was our son? When I held him for the first time and said "Hey, little guy," he opened his eyes, and I knew.

Darrin and I didn't have a name picked out. We hadn't even packed our bags for the hospital. Although I'm fairly certain we were the only couple in our Lamaze class who purchased the suggested paint roller (to help ease the pain of contractions!), Darrin walked downstairs an hour later to inform the "How to Take Care of a Baby" class instructor that we wouldn't be attending the class. No time to practice on plastic babies—our real one had come. After we resettled in the room, Darrin drove home and washed blood off the carpet, packed a few things, and returned to the hospital with our *10,000 Baby Names* book. As we talked about all that had transpired, it became clear we would name our son Jonathan: "gift of God" in Hebrew.

Life is a gift from God. Our beating hearts and the air that fills our lungs are gifts from God. So is our inborn capacity to connect with Him. From the beginning of time, God's intention for us as image bearers has been to have an intimate relationship with Him. While this doesn't mean we won't have trials and disappointments, God desires to reveal Himself so that we can know Him and trust Him with every aspect of our lives, no matter what. A soul-anchoring faith that enables us to weather our inevitable challenges and heart-aches is grounded in an accurate understanding of what He is like.

The Comfort of God's Character

We live in an increasingly narcissistic generation of selfies, and often we approach God's Word with the attitude of "What does this passage tell me about *me*? What does this mean for *my* life?" But if we approach the Bible as if we're reading a fortune cookie or horoscope, we miss so much. God gifted us with His Word so that we can know who *He* is. No other book is described as "living and active and sharper than any two-edged sword, and piercing as far as the division of soul and spirit, of both joints and marrow, and able to judge the thoughts and intentions of the heart" (Hebrews 4:12). God reveals Himself through creation and sometimes through other people, but created things give only a partial picture. It's like studying a famous painting: we can appreciate and perceive certain nuances of the artist by looking at his work, but hearing directly from the artist with regard to the thoughts and motivations behind each masterpiece is the only way to truly understand the art.

As we read Scripture, better questions to ask are "What does this passage teach me about *God*? What do I learn about His will, His heart, and His ways?" Each time Jesus was tempted in the wilderness, He responded with "It is written . . ." He continually looked to His Father and the Scriptures for guidance, perspective, and strength. Surrender happens as we become captured by who God is. He can do anything. He knows everything. He loves us. These qualities are braided together. An all-knowing God who is loving but not powerful would be impotent. An all-knowing and all-powerful God who is not loving would be terrifying. An all-powerful God who is loving but not all knowing would be unhelpful.

Let's say I fall off a cliff. And let's say my mom hears my cries and peers over the edge and sees me clinging to a branch. She knows I'm in trouble, and without question she loves me and would do anything for me. But due to the fact that she is shorter than me, weighs less than me, and is a grandma and therefore in the "older" category (sorry, Mom), in this scenario she would be unable to help.

Now replace my wonderful but probably-can't-even-lift-my-thigh mom with some sinister mass murderer who happens to despise women. My cries for help lead him to look over the edge. He knows I'm in trouble and has the strength to pull me up, but I would be foolish to let go and entrust my life to him if I know he couldn't care less about my well-being and would rather see me plunge to my death.

Same scenario, but the person this time is *my* person, my husband. A modern-day Jean Valjean who carried a refrigerator on his back up the stairs to our second-floor apartment in West L.A., Darrin is the strongest man I know. Does he love me? Why yes, even though I drive him nuts. Is he strong enough? Last I checked, I still weigh less than a fridge. But what if he's out with his friends watching a football game while I dangle over the precipice? He loves me and is strong enough to help, but if he doesn't know my situation, he cannot come to my aid.

The reason we can trust God is that He is all the things we need, all at the same time, and His character never changes.

All Knowing

The prophet Isaiah penned words in an attempt to describe God, but even the rich imagery in chapter 40 depicting God's magnificence cannot adequately capture all of who He is.

Regarding God's omniscience, Isaiah wrote in verse 26,

Lift up your eyes on high
And see who has created these stars,
The One who leads forth their host by number,
He calls them all by name;
Because of the greatness of His might and the strength of His
    power,
Not one of them is missing.

God knows the names of each and every star. He knows how many hairs are on our heads (Luke 12:7). He doesn't need to be taught anything. Nothing is hidden from His sight. He knows all that can be known. He is never surprised. Scripture states, "Your Father knows what you need before you ask Him" (Matthew 6:8). And in Psalm 139:4 David wrote, "Even before a word is on my tongue, behold, O LORD, you know it altogether" (ESV).

When God says He is all knowing, or omniscient, it means He knows everything. He orchestrates whom we meet and where we have been and will go.

A college student from Texas waited on a bench outside a store in Frankfurt, Germany. The rest of her team picked up last-minute supplies before heading to their final destination for their summer missions outreach in eastern Europe. A woman walked past the student and stopped.

"Excuse me, but I think I know you."

The woman had an Australian accent, and the student had never set foot in Australia. The student said, "I'm sorry. I think you've mistaken me for someone else."

But the woman persisted. Suddenly, she remembered. "Were you in Hawaii last summer?" The student had spent the summer in Hawaii on a summer mission to receive training in evangelism and discipleship. "You came up to me on the beach and shared a small booklet with me about how to know God personally, and I've been thinking about it ever since."

God knows every step we will take during our lifetimes, but many of us from Western cultures wrestle with His omniscience. Western thinking, based in Greek thought, is dualistic, either/or, linear, and sequential. Eastern thinking is more pluralistic, and/also, with more circular reasoning that enables one to hold conflicting views in tension. People with Western thinking sometimes wonder about the role of prayer. If God knows what I'm going to say before I say it and what I need before I ask, then what is the point of prayer?

Question: What can I tell an all-knowing God?

Answer: Nothing.

When people with Eastern thinking and values hear that God knows everything, including what we are going to say before we say it and what we need before we ask, the answer to the same question looks different.

Question: What can I tell an all-knowing God?

Answer: Anything.

Such joy and comfort come through being completely known. From this perspective prayer changes from getting *something* to knowing and communing with *Someone*.

This is just one example of how our culture influences the lens through which we read and study Scripture. The culture at the time the Scriptures were written was Eastern. This is why we can read both lament and praise side by side in the same psalm. By studying Scripture in community and with the lens of people who don't share our same culture and context, we gain a richer understanding of who God is and what He is like.

All Powerful

When God says He is all powerful, or omnipotent, it means nothing is too hard for Him. He spoke, and the worlds came into being. This required no effort. All resources belong to Him. He has unlimited time and energy.

> Do you not know? Have you not heard?
> The Everlasting God, the LORD, the Creator of the ends of the earth
> Does not become weary or tired.
> His understanding is inscrutable. (Isaiah 40:28)

Several years ago I was in a Japanese church in Kyoto, Japan, sitting with my two small children in the cry room, which was encased in glass above the sanctuary. I found the unexpected air-conditioning a welcome relief from the ninety-five-degree temperatures with matching 95 percent humidity. The rest of our US summer missions team sat in the chairs set up in orderly rows in the main room we overlooked, without air-conditioning, fanning themselves with their flimsy programs.

Jonathan, age four and three-quarters, blended in with the rest of the Japanese preschoolers as he lost himself in a picture book. Michael, our seventeen-month-old, joined the rest of the toddlers playing with a small pile of toys. Leaning up against a wall, I looked around at the other moms. Despite the language barrier, we shared the universal look of young-mom fatigue along with triumph at making it out the door to church with our little ones in tow.

One of the moms quietly sat down next to me and asked me a question in Japanese. I answered with the one Japanese phrase I know, *"Wakarimasen,"* which means "I don't understand," and pointed to our group below. She covered her mouth and laughed with her eyes in understanding, then asked in English for my name and about our group. She apologized profusely for her poor English, which, like that of most Japanese college graduates, was quite excellent. We pointed out our children to each other and shared their names and ages. I assured her how impressed I was with her English and asked about her spiritual journey.

Then, as if an invisible cocoon of privacy surrounded us, she started to explain how a missionary family had lived on her street. As a little girl she'd attended weekly Bible studies to practice English. She learned that God loved her and wanted a relationship with her, so she gave her heart to Jesus.

Then she shared that her father started sexually abusing her when she was in junior high school. When she moved away for college, she experienced deep depression. The dormitories in Japan house freshmen alone in small rooms. Isolated and despairing, she decided one night to take her life, finally putting an end to her pain. Right before she was going to end her life, she cried out loud to God, "God, if You are real and You love me, You have to show me now."

She randomly flipped open the Bible she brought with her to

school and read the first verse she saw: "'I have loved you,' says the LORD" (Malachi 1:2). With tears in her eyes, she went on to tell me, "A few years later God helped me forgive my father. When that happened, I gave God complete control of my life. I know deep in my heart that if God could help me forgive my dad, then He truly can do anything."

We might think of God as "out there," where He's handling the big stuff of the universe rather than concerning Himself with our little lives. But as the Japanese woman's experience attests, this all-powerful aspect of God can be very personal. Isaiah wrote, "O LORD, You are my God; I will exalt You, I will give thanks to Your name; for You have worked wonders, plans formed long ago, with perfect faithfulness" (Isaiah 25:1).

All Loving

When God says He is all loving, it means He is good. His intentions are good. His motives toward us are good. His love is so great that He would rather die than live without us. "He who did not spare His own Son, but delivered Him over for us all, how will He not also with Him freely give us all things?" (Romans 8:32).

I have come to a profound understanding of God's love through becoming a mom. I love Darrin, and I love my family and friends, but a whole new type of love opened up for me when I became a mother. The love I have for my kids is intense and protective. I wouldn't hesitate to risk my life if anyone threatened to hurt my children. You hear about moms who lift trucks to rescue their kids pinned underneath. Momma bear love is *fierce*.

I remember experiencing this maternal intensity when our middle son, Michael, as a preschooler, slipped while climbing on our kitchen counters and almost bit clear through his tongue; when baby Julia ended up in the emergency room due to a febrile seizure; and when our oldest child, Jonathan, hit his head on the coffee table when he was eighteen months old. As a new mom on my first trip to the emergency room, I could feel the adrenaline coursing through my veins. I wouldn't have had a problem throwing the doctor across the room if he had tried anything stupid.

After examining the cut, the doctor determined that Jonathan would need stitches. He instructed me to hold my young son's upper body still and my friend who joined us to hold his legs. The first shot used to numb the area over Jonathan's eye didn't work, so they had to give him another. I forced back tears in order to stay strong for my little boy. I ached to see him scared, helpless, and in pain. I loved him so much; I would have taken a thousand stitches for him to not have to experience his own. Then it hit—Jesus did exactly that for me. He suffered and died in my place. In the same moment I also realized in a brand-new way how God takes no pleasure in my pain. When I'm in pain, He never leaves. He is right there with me. When life makes no sense, I need to choose to fall back on the truth of His unchanging love.

Abraham displayed this kind of radical trust in God's character. In Genesis 21 and 22, we read of God's fulfillment of His promise to Abraham when the centenarian's wife, Sarah, gave birth (at age ninety!) to the child God had promised to them. Isaac was a miracle—a living and breathing, walking and talking impossibility. Every day of Isaac's life reminded Abraham and Sarah of God's faithfulness, perfect provision, and ultimate sovereignty. But after making good on His covenant promise, when this precious only son became a young man, God asked Abraham to sacrifice Isaac on an altar. In faith Abraham obeyed, trusting that God would not renege on His promise but would somehow raise Isaac from the dead (Hebrews 11:17–19).

Abraham surrendered to God's will, and Isaac did as well. Isaac could have overpowered his older, frail father, but he let Abraham tie him down and watched as his loving father lifted his knife to kill him as an offering to God. Isaac loved and trusted both his father, Abraham, and his God, Yahweh. When Abraham demonstrated his love for God by offering up his only son, God spared the son and provided the sacrifice.

In His own Son's case, God demonstrated His great love for you and me by *not* sparing Jesus. Jesus, too, could have sought to preserve His life by leaving His sleeping friends in the garden and running away to a distant country. Instead, He wrestled and finally surrendered, praying, "Not My will, but Yours be done" (Luke 22:42).

Abraham, Isaac, and Jesus knew they could rest secure in God the Father's hands because they knew God loved them deeply. We, too, can live completely surrendered only when we take in and live out this truth: *God loves us so much that He gave His only Son to save us.* No sacrifice we make, no matter how dear, will ever trump the sacrifice made on the cross by our Savior. Our response to this great love should be to give ourselves back to Him, to offer up our lives as a living sacrifice (Romans 12:1–2).

We will come to this crossroads of trust over and over; knowing God loves us doesn't automatically make surrender easy. But in the midst of whatever life presents to us, we can safely let go and rest in God's great love. God is after our hearts and access to all areas of our lives. Our ability to say yes to Him is the path to life.

Looking back at the book of Esther, notice that God is not mentioned once in all ten chapters, but His hand of providence and provision is seen throughout her story. God is always at work behind the scenes. Many of us won't know the full explanation of why circumstances turned out as they did until we see God face to face. But in the here and now, no matter our circumstance, God is near, and He is good. Still, even when we know life is found in surrendering to Him, we sometimes have difficulty prying open our hands. We hold on, white knuckled, to our expectations and plans, or we are lulled into passivity or spiritual apathy. Sometimes our fears of running out or of needing to rely on others drive us to spend our energies on acquiring more and stashing away our resources, claiming them as ours alone. In the following chapters we will look more closely at our self-preserving ways. To cultivate a willing heart, we need to look at what keeps us from opening our hands.

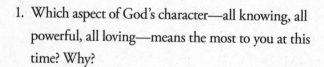

Questions for Reflection and Discussion

1. Which aspect of God's character—all knowing, all powerful, all loving—means the most to you at this time? Why?

2. Consider an all-knowing God who orchestrates whom we meet and where we have been and will go. What thoughts and feelings does this bring up for you?

3. How does knowing that God is omniscient affect your prayer life?

4. Think of a time when the all-powerful aspect of God felt personal to you. How did you see His omnipotence at work in your life?

5. What stood out to you in this chapter about God's love in the lives of Abraham, Isaac, and Jesus?

6. Reflect on a time when your circumstances made it hard to trust that God is good. How did you work through this?

7. "God is after our hearts and access to all areas of our lives. Our ability to say yes to Him is the path to life." What are your thoughts about this statement? Is there an area of your life you find difficult to surrender to God? If so, why?

8. If you know people whose culture or ethnicity is different
   from your own, ask them how they view what Scripture says
   about God as all knowing, all powerful, and all loving. In
   what ways are their perspectives different from yours?

PART 2

WHAT GETS
IN THE WAY

3

Apathy and Entitlement

If you can once get him to the point of thinking that
"religion is all very well up to a point," you can feel quite
happy about his soul. A moderated religion is as good
for us as no religion at all—and more amusing.

—C. S. Lewis, *The Screwtape Letters*

G rowing up culturally Buddhist and raised in an immigrant
home, I learned about American holidays at school. Christmas
held no spiritual significance and revolved around presents and Santa
Claus. Easter had something to do with a giant white bunny, jelly beans,
and colorful hidden eggs. Saint Patrick's Day meant green shakes at
McDonald's, something about pinching, and little troublemakers called
leprechauns who had brown beards, wore green, and spoke with funny
accents. That was the extent of my knowledge of Christian holidays.

Then, during my sophomore year of high school, a friend I sat
next to in math class underwent a notable change in her disposition.
Intrigued, I asked Jean the secret of her newfound "glow."

"Did you become a vegetarian or something?"

"What do you mean?"

"There's something different about you. I see it. It's like you're glowing."

"Wow. You really see a difference? You really want to know?"

I nodded.

"Well, Viv, I became a Christian."

"What do you mean? Did you start going to church?"

"No. I have a personal relationship with Jesus now. He died to forgive my sins, and now I'm born again and made new. The glow is from my new life in Christ."

Oh no. Disappointment filled me from head to toe. Jean was funny and smart. How could she get duped into becoming a weird Jesus freak? But over the course of the year, the change in her stuck and she continued to transform before my eyes. God worked in her life in specific and unexplainable ways. She explained how the void within human beings couldn't be filled with relationships, shopping, or awards and achievements. God made people with a God-shaped vacuum only He can fill, and our restless, unquenchable hearts cannot find rest until they reconnect with the God who made them.

My heart felt restless. Even as a teenager I could already see the futility of going after bigger, brighter, better. The temporary thrill of winning an award or buying something new to wear could not relieve the emptiness I felt inside. But I had questions. Barrels of questions. Why did God allow evil? How do we know the Bible isn't mythology? What about other religions? Why does Jesus claim to be the only way to God? What about people who never hear about Jesus? I couldn't deny my skepticism, yet I knew this world held breathtaking beauty alongside horrendous acts of violence. If God didn't create beauty and goodness, then who did?

I started going to church and attending the youth group, mostly to check out the cute boys at first. But over the course of the year, I asked my questions and learned that I wasn't expected to have blind faith. As I learned and studied, I became captivated by the person of Jesus, who lived, walked, acted, and spoke words of radical hope. His invitation to enter a relationship with the God of heaven and to belong to His spiritual family proved irresistible. The summer before my junior year of high school, I gave my heart and life to Jesus.

At first I didn't know much about what that really meant, but I knew Christians had Bibles, so I went to the mall and bought one at the bookstore. I thumbed through and found strange names and places I had trouble pronouncing, lists of who begat whom begat whom, and measurements of temples and repetitive sayings about offerings and evil kings. Some sections seemed formatted like Shakespeare's sonnets; some books were long, and others were only a few pages. No matter how much I read, very little made sense. Much of the content tasted like a bowl of stale cornflakes.

Christians prayed, so I tried closing my eyes and praying. I remembered seeing in a movie people making the sign of the cross, so I did the same in hopes it would add some extra luck to my prayers—like blowing on the dice before releasing during Monopoly. Sadly, I'd drift off to sleep, start thinking about my friends and their relationship woes, be distracted by a top-forty song that would pop into my head, or remember something to add to my to-do list. Honestly, I wondered how my one-sided ramblings and requests made any difference.

If I woke up in time on Sunday mornings, I would drive myself to church and cry through every song during worship. The lyrics expressed the longing of my heart—I wanted to know God and trust Him, to love Him and live for Him. But then I would drive home and life would go back to how it had been. I would return to my selfish ways and take matters into my own hands. I remained focused on *my* needs and *my* expectations, *my* way of doing, thinking, and living. This Jesus thing wasn't really working for me. I started to wonder if only a small handful of elite, special people enjoyed vibrant Christianity. Maybe it just wasn't attainable for ordinary people like me. I had yet to learn how God provided His Spirit for everyone, not just a select few.

For each of us the Christian life is one of divine appointments, character change, answered prayer, and joy and serenity that don't always match our circumstances. In other words, living for Jesus is an *extraordinary* journey, available to all who live with open hands and willing hearts. What does this way of life look like?

Well Above Average

If you happened across a frog while you were walking on the side of the road, you wouldn't start yelling wildly, "Oh wow! It hops far, it eats flies, and its throat balloons out!" Those are traits of normal frogs. But when it comes to our faith, we get excited by Christians who walk their talk. "Oh wow! She invited her coworker to church, she shared and led her neighbor to Christ, and she disciples other women!" We may think these are superstar Christians when they are simply being normal Christians.

So why do many believers settle for being *average* Christians instead of embodying all that being a *normal* Christian entails? Though all Christians are indwelt by the Holy Spirit, not all Christians are filled and empowered by the Spirit. Average Christians often aren't much different from nonbelievers in their words and actions. In fact, many nonbelievers live with integrity, generosity, and compassion, putting believers to shame by their example.

Part of the problem is that many professing Christians, especially in North America, live as spiritual weekend warriors. Apart from getting up and out the door for worship, listening to teaching, and snacking during fellowship hour, our lives look no different from anyone else's living anywhere along our street. Monday morning arrives and life takes over. Perhaps we say a quick prayer before eating a meal and a sleepy "God bless so and so" as we drift off to sleep, but for the most part we go through the motions without our faith intersecting our day-to-day lives. With our eternal destiny secure, many believers become passive and complacent. But God created in each of us a soul shaped to experience and care deeply for things bigger than the little corners we occupy.

In the masterfully written satirical classic *The Screwtape Letters,* two demons who set out to undermine a Christian exchange missives. The elder demon, Screwtape, is training his nephew, Wormwood, in the ways of human nature and responses of believers. He encourages Wormwood to lull them into passivity and a don't-rock-the-boat religion. The outcome of such apathy and complacency would be a life that, over years, steadily veered off course.

Esther lived with this posture of passivity after she took residence in the king's palace. All her needs and wants were provided for: the best food, wine, clothing, and jewels, along with maidens and attendants.

Her life consisted of mud baths and face masks and all the comforts of palace life. In Esther 1 we read about the wealth and opulence in Xerxes's kingdom. Before Esther enters the scene, we read of a party lasting 180 days—a full six months—to show off all his expensive stuff, like the finest wine served in goblets made of pure gold. Esther ends up being just another pretty possession. Young girls were expendable commodities for the king to take out for test-drives, just like a new sports car. (I feel furious just thinking about the circumstances surrounding those teenage girls!)

Esther patterned her life to follow the man in charge of the harem, Hegai, and his instructions (Esther 2:15). Over and over Esther deferred to men—Mordecai, Hegai, and Xerxes—and lived a bonbon-popping life. In contrast, other women in the Old Testament chose to obey God over the edicts of their rulers. The Hebrew midwives feared God and did not follow instructions to kill the Hebrew baby boys (Exodus 1:17). Moses's mom hid him as a newborn. When he grew too big, she placed him in a basket and floated him down the Nile. His sister, Miriam, followed the basket all the way into the arms of the pharaoh's daughter and offered to find a wet nurse for him, which returned Moses to his mom for a few years (2:2–9). Rahab hid the Israelite spies in Jericho (Joshua 2). And these are but a few of the upstanding women role models in the Old Testament. They honored God regardless of the cost, knowing their lives might be on the line. They demonstrated active faith.

Now, most of us do not live in the lap of luxury with endless spa days. We don't have maidens nearby to order our schedules and iron our clothes. We legitimately struggle with mounds of bills, piles of laundry, and the work set before us day in, day out. We can, however, fall prey to a going-through-the-motions kind of faith. Do we settle for "pew warming" and toss a few dollars in the offering plate when it goes by? Do we open the Bible on any day other than Sunday at church? Sometimes church becomes a cultural or social place where we make connections or where our children can be influenced by "good people." Many of my friends who grew up in immigrant homes found church to be a place to gather for camaraderie, shared culture, language, and food and a resource for tips on navigating life in a new country. Today many attend church to find dating prospects or business leads. Consumer Christianity drives our demand for church to be entertaining. The search for the best preachers and most moving worship keeps some of us perpetually "church hopping."

We can get spiritually numbed by filling our schedules with endless activities interspersed with small dollops of Jesus. "Just be a good person" becomes our motto. Our daily lives and relationships remain unaffected as we make God a fancy hood ornament or a superficial accessory. Spiritual apathy can be an obstacle particularly for those who grew up attending church and know all the Bible stories by heart. Their very familiarity with the Christian faith can put them at risk of falling into a spiritual stupor. Others become disillusioned with the hypocrisy they see in those who claim to be Christians. Left with a bad taste in their mouths, they withdraw from church and from fellowship with other believers.

It's important for us to ask ourselves where we stand because the outcome of going through the motions can lead us far from our original proximity to Jesus. Bobbing in the currents of the ocean, we aren't cognizant of the strength of the undertow as we swim and splash. Not until we stop and look back to shore to establish our bearings do we realize how far we've drifted. Our beach umbrellas and towels, small in the distance, do not grow legs and move; we are the ones who've pulled away, often completely unaware. Over time our objective can shift from living in vital relationship with God to pursuing comfort and material abundance.

The Prosperity Gospel

I am such a sucker for "the next best thing." Bring on the latest fads: the Instant Pot, the Bullet Journal, essential oils, chia seeds, Voxer, MUJI pens, washi tape, the paleo diet, Fitbit, and all the coffee paraphernalia—the AeroPress, the Hario pour-over system, burr grinders. The list of fads and material goodies goes on and on. Remember Creative Memories? "The Rachel" haircut? Grunge? The PalmPilot? Denim overalls from Gap? The computer that came in a black-and-white cow-print box? Each comes with promises: time or financial savings, weight loss, better organization, enhanced flavor, or greater health. "I believe! I believe!" I say, as I pull out my wallet and sign up in hopes that these items will deliver all the goodness they promise.

There's nothing necessarily wrong with the next best thing, but if we're not careful, we can find ourselves focusing on things created rather than on the Creator. The idea of #blessed in modern times has taken on a life of its own. It's all too tempting to reduce God to a cosmic vending machine. Many sit under a teaching emphasizing that enough prayer, enough giving, and enough faith will yield God's blessing, especially in the arenas of financial wealth and physical health. This potentially greed-driven focus of "name it, claim it" discounts so many stories in Scripture of faithful followers who did *not* experience the outcomes for which they hoped and prayed.

In fact, in the Old Testament God set up if-then agreements with the Israelites called covenants. In a variety of ways, God explained, "If you obey, then I will bless." In Genesis 12–50, God established the Abrahamic covenant, promising the land and descendants as numerous as the stars. The Mosaic covenant (Exodus–Deuteronomy) lays out the blessings God would give if the Israelites obeyed, along with the disasters disobedience would bring. The book of Joshua records God's faithfulness to the covenant. The book of Judges records Israel's unfaithfulness to the covenant. God put covenants in place to reveal Himself to His people and deepen a relationship with them. And all of it pointed to the new covenant in which God would finally dwell with His people as Immanuel, "God with us." The objective of the covenants was *not* blessings; it was *relationship*.

The subtle infiltration of the prosperity gospel also manifests itself when we bump up against any type of trial. The jarring of illness or other difficulty exposes our expectations of a life of ease. Displayed on the shelves of grocery stores and drugstores is our clear intolerance for pain. We find row after row of antidotes to combat pain from headaches, cramps, flu symptoms, muscle aches, and wounds. We often live with an attitude of entitlement and feel exasperated when we experience any unpleasant symptom. Similarly, our vending-machine prayers demand that God respond immediately, and like trying to free a stuck candy bar, we start kicking at any sign of delay. After all, being a child of God should entitle us to a fast pass to the front of the line, and answers to our prayers ought to come quickly and easily. We expect obedience to yield blessing, failing to see the full picture of God at work through the good *and* the hard. We numb emotional pain through endless activity, alcohol and prescription drugs, and pornography and sex addictions, as well as seemingly more socially acceptable addictions to food, shopping, cleaning, work, ministry, social media, and gaming. For many the presence of pain equals the absence of blessing, but the longer we walk the earth, the more we find pain and disappointment woven into life in a fallen world. None of us are exempt from suffering. Even those who seem to live charmed lives have internal struggles. Often our pain is what brings us to recognize our need for God. In my own life, and for the vast number of people I know, pain is an instrument God uses to grow character and to deepen our relationship with Him. God wants us to know Him and not just know about Him.

When life is about acquiring and seeking an ever-elusive comfort level, we begin a dangerous drift toward wanting God's blessings and gifts but not being interested in God Himself. Here's a place for us to begin some self-evaluation: What is our goal? Is our relationship with God based on the benefits we receive from Him? Is our dedication linked to what we can get?

A Matter of Perspective

The grip of apathy and entitlement gets loosened by challenging our perceptions through proximity, humility, and generosity. We break down barriers and build bridges through involvement in our communities and beyond as we intentionally seek opportunities to contribute and receive in places where we normally wouldn't participate.

Proximity requires spending time in other communities and cultures. Left to myself, I start thinking everyone lives, eats, thinks, and acts just like me. But each time I move away from the familiar and out into the wider world, I realize how God is vast, infinite, and multidimensional. His creation reflects who He is, and I don't want to put constraints on knowing Him and *all* the people He loves. Awareness of others who don't have access to clean water, housing, education, health care, or a place to call home is the first step in opening our hearts and hands and releasing the resources God has given us.

This is not merely visiting a foreign location as a tourist or visitor while remaining in a position of power. Too often in missions work, the sending organization retains a posture of dominance and superiority because of socioeconomic inequality. This mind-set of "helping those people" places those with less in an inferior position. Those of us with resources can shift dangerously to becoming self-righteous, judgmental, and elitist and viewing those who are marginalized through distorted lenses. A posture of humility allows for mutuality and true partnership because it helps to equalize the balance of power.[2] I remember having lunch with Una Mulale, a brilliant pediatric critical care doctor from Botswana. She shared a story of some well-meaning missionaries who wanted to help an African tribe. The village needed food. The missionaries noticed some fertile land next to the river, so they decided to plant tomatoes. What they didn't know because they failed to ask was the reason why the fertile soil remained unfarmed by the locals. Aggressive and deadly hippopotamuses lived in the river and would come out of the water and prey on children helping in the fields. The work of the missionaries proved unhelpful because of their attitude of thinking they knew best what the community needed.

We all have perception problems. Situated on the wall directly in front of me in my office is a world map. Russia looks larger than Africa, but in reality Africa can hold *two* Russias. Fifty-four countries comprise the enormous continent of Africa, which is bigger than the landmasses of the following countries *combined:* China, India, United States, Mexico, Peru, Spain, France, Sweden, Japan, Papua New Guinea, Germany, Italy, Norway, New Zealand, Nepal, the United Kingdom, Greece, and Bangladesh. And just to give more perspective: *ten* European countries can fit inside the state of Texas with room to spare!

Take a moment and scroll in your mind through pictures you've seen of stunning geography. Our world is full of different climates, landscapes, food sources, and cultures. People bear God's image and display His beauty and grandeur through language, art, structures, music, inventions, foods, skills, and customs. Let those images of places and people remind us of this truth: God is *not* an American. Though that is funny to write and read, I often need this reminder.

As someone born and raised in the United States reading and speaking English, I'm tempted to start thinking the Bible should be read from left to right across the page—that somehow this way is the "right" way, just like driving on the right side of the road with the steering wheel on the left side is the "right" way. But 287 million Christians currently live in Asia, compared to 267 million in North America, and many Asian believers open the Bible from what we consider the back of the book and read the Scriptures in columns up and down from the right page to the left.

We also need to be careful to not impose modern Western culture and perspectives on the texts we read. Americans don't have a corner on the market when it comes to theology and doctrine. We forget that women and men studied the Scriptures and sought to walk faithfully with God since the first century AD. We forget that God has always been at work revealing Himself faithfully all around the world to those who seek truth. We forget that Jesus never spoke a word of English when He walked the earth. Sadly, many people today probably wouldn't warmly welcome Jesus if He visited our churches on a Sunday simply because a bearded Middle Eastern man is often perceived as dangerous.

In the midst of our tendency toward division and separation, I'm encouraged by the many believers who are actively investing their lives in building bridges across cultural divides. After the 1992 Los Angeles riots, the ministry of Cru Inner City partnered with community leader John Perkins to find a long-term solution, and the concept of the S.A.Y. (Save. America's. Youth.) Yes! Center was born. They challenged local churches to make a twelve-year commitment to adopt kids in their neighborhood into an after-school program and to stay with the entire group from first grade through graduation from high school.

Our longtime friends Sarah and Scott Yetter live in downtown Los Angeles in the Pico-Union area. In 2001 they founded a youth development program at their church in the middle of this inner-city community where Scott serves as the English-language pastor. As one of fourteen centers in the Los Angeles area, the Pico-Union S.A.Y. Yes! Center began with fifteen students and three volunteer staff and over time has grown to as many as forty students and nine creatively paid staff. Their firm commitment to keeping the ratio of mentor to child at 1:5 means the kids have the benefit of personalized instruction and input. Some mentors stay with the same kids over several years. Now students who graduated from the program have returned to invest back into the community. Sarah and Scott's commitment to remain in proximity and raise their family in this community has built trust and credibility and yielded the blessing of lives transformed.

The choice to invest their lives in others can seem costly, but Sarah shares so beautifully some of her process:

> Here is life for me, not because I'm "needed" here in any Messiah-type way, but because I've thrown in my lot with my neighbors, and how they're doing is intimately bound to how I'm doing. That's why S.A.Y. Yes! is in my life blood, because it will take a community, one that includes holders of graduate degrees and makers of killer tamales and metalworkers who started working at age ten—all of us—to launch our kids to greatness. Would I live in this neighborhood, wearing it like some urban badge of honor, and not give my very life to share life and resources with these young champions? To live and love and risk here means, for me at least, to keep my doors open so that life is shared when it's both convenient and not convenient for me; it means our family is sometimes misunderstood and not rushing to explain ourselves or post on social media why we're cool or "with it"; it means we're stretched far out of our comfort zones to places where we cry together or bite at each other and we must continually rush back to that well of grace and forgiveness in Jesus.

A police sergeant responsible for patrolling their neighborhood shared how the police department noticed a decline in violence, crime, and gang activity after the center opened. Would-be taggers were told by neighborhood youth *not* to vandalize the church because "this church loves the community." This is such a beautiful example of being salt and light. The faithful, humble, generous love Sarah and Scott display and their commitment to live in proximity to the community have forged deep friendships and opened avenues for people from suburban areas to also become involved. Partner churches continue to send their youth to participate in inner-city ministry.

Stereotypes and prejudices can be broken when we choose to bind our lives together with others and allow genuine relationships to form over time. Individuals are changed and families and communities are transformed when God directs our paths to cross with the paths of others all around us.

As we ask God to open our eyes, He is faithful to expand our hearts as we form connections orchestrated by Him. Rather than walking around people, we are called to move toward fellow image bearers of our God and love them in radical ways.

Questions for Reflection and Discussion

1. If you are using this book in a discussion group, spend about five minutes per person sharing your story of becoming a Christian. Was there a particular person involved in your coming to know Jesus? If so, what role did that individual play?

2. In what ways do you live differently from the nonbelievers you know? If you don't see a difference, what are some ways you could ask God to help you become more like Jesus?

3. Have you experienced a time of apathy and a going-through-the-motions type of faith? If so, how did you move out of it?

4. What does it mean to you to demonstrate an active faith? What does it look like in your actions and relationships?

5. What do you think about the statement "It's all too tempting to reduce God to a cosmic vending machine"? Have you or someone you know been guilty of this? If so, how has it played out?

6. Think of a time when difficulty or suffering exposed your expectation that your life should be easier or more blessed. Were you disillusioned or angry with God? If so, how did you work through this?

7. Consider the statement "God is *not* an American." How have you imposed your cultural bias on what it means to be a Christian?

8. Where might you contribute and receive in an area you normally wouldn't participate? What might it look like for you to get out of your comfort zone?

4

Self-Reliance

The Christian life is what you do when you realize you
can do nothing.

—DALLAS WILLARD

The metal creaked at the hinges as I forced open the door that never
completely shut. Hopping from one foot to the other on the hot
sidewalk, I made my way to the mailbox, which tilted to the left,
flimsy and rusted. I made a mental note to add "replace mailbox" to
the growing honey-do list at our first home.

I eagerly removed the contents, which amounted to pizza coupons
and two pieces of "real" mail. I ripped open the first envelope, praying
it would contain a donation to support our upcoming missions trip to
Japan. Darrin and I had learned that less than 1 percent of the population there had a relationship with Jesus. A decade earlier hundreds of
college students with Cru (formerly Campus Crusade for Christ) in-
vested their summers in missions to Japan. Many current-day Japanese
pastors, Christian leaders, and professors were introduced to Jesus

through these summer missions. Over time the number of student missionaries from California dwindled to zero. As God burdened our hearts, we began dreaming and praying for a team to help us kick-start a new partnership with Japan. God faithfully brought together a small group of college students to join us, and our departure date was now ten days away.

We had sent out our monthly ministry newsletter, sharing about our desire to minister in Japan and inviting our donors to join our team through prayer and financial support. We relied on donations from churches, individuals, and families for all the necessary funds to live and minister.

In the first envelope I opened was a check for $50. (For those raised in the Venmo/online banking era, a check is a piece of paper written to transfer funds between bank accounts. It was popular back in the day!) I was grateful for the financial gift, but I panicked as I read the note in the second envelope. The letter informed us that a donor who normally gave $500 a month would no longer be supporting us. So far only $175 had come in of the $10,000 needed for our family of four to minister in Japan.

I ran into the house to show Darrin the letter from our ministry partner. Darrin is the calm, steady one in all types of emergencies. Nerves of steel. I am just not wired to be calm. At all.

"Darrin, I can't believe so few people have responded to our missions opportunity. Maybe Japan doesn't seem like a mission field to them. Maybe we should only do missions in developing nations. Do you think we should've sent two letters? We. Are. Supposed. To. Leave. In. Ten. Days!"

I paced in circles around the living room, throwing my arms into the air and grabbing my hair in distress while pacing some more. Darrin, meanwhile, sat calmly at the dining room table.

"How can you sit there so calm?"

Of course. He was praying. So I joined him. And then I couldn't focus, so I stopped.

"Darrin, we could lose our house. I mean, we don't have enough support for the summer, and now we're losing five hundred dollars in monthly donations!"

Darrin looked over at me and said matter-of-factly, "Viv, I think the Lord can still provide all we need."

Argh! The gift of faith! How frustrating. Argh!

Darrin remained confident of God's provision. I, on the other hand, felt absolutely desperate. So I decided to fast and pray for the entire weekend. My prayer was simple: "Father, You know how I have a hard time trusting. I need to see You bring in at least a thousand of our needed ten thousand dollars. If you bring in the thousand dollars, I'll be okay to go to Japan and will trust You with the rest."

The calendar I made for Jonathan and Michael to show how many more sleeps until our departure date counted down into the single digits. Our suitcases lay open on the living room floor, contents strewn about. One afternoon the doorbell rang. I peered through the peephole. A man in an official postal uniform stood on our porch holding a bin. Puzzled, I opened the door.

"Excuse me, are you the lady of the house?"

"Yes."

"Ma'am, this bin of mail has been waiting for you at the post office. I happened to see it because you're on my route this week, so I thought I'd bring it to you."

Confused, I responded, "I know we put a hold on our mail while we were visiting my parents. But we received a big stack when we returned, so I thought everything had been delivered."

"Well, apparently not. This bin has been sitting in the post office."

I thanked the postal worker, took the large bin, and gently shut the door and slid to the ground. Tears filled my eyes as I looked at all the envelopes. I started ripping open one after another. Notes of encouragement, increased monthly pledges, excitement about our summer mission, and checks totaling more than the $1,000 I had asked the Lord to provide.

Viv, I sensed God saying, *you think you know how to do this missions thing because you've been on Cru staff for a decade. You and Darrin have led team after team, and you have raised support so many times: write a letter, include envelopes and response cards, pray, and run to the mailbox to collect what you need. But I am sending you to a country that is 99 percent unbelievers. You can't just go through the motions, thinking you know how all this works. You are engaging in a spiritual battle, and I want your reliance to be on* Me.

Wow. Nailed right between the eyes, pierced straight through the heart. Of course. It made sense now. The mail delivery mix-up served to wake me from my slumber. I needed to be jolted into relying on God. I needed fresh faith. God in His kindness and mercy allowed only some mail, including the letter about our large monthly donation, to come through to make me desperate to pray.

I'm sure that you, too, have stories about trying to do God's will while using your own know-how and willpower. It's unsustainable, isn't it? Living the Christian life in our own strength isn't just hard; it's impossible. We can be doing all the right things, but without reliance on the Holy Spirit, we are limited by on-our-own finite and fallible strength and resources.

Reliance on the Spirit

When I first started walking with God in high school, I tried to do all the Christian activities but found my conduct in some ways getting worse after having my eyes opened to right and wrong. Before knowing Christ, I could simply lower my standards and still feel okay about myself. Now I really wanted to change and be in the center of God's will, but I felt defeated and frustrated. Finally I concluded this "Christian thing" would be another passing teenage phase.

After our move to Hong Kong before my senior year of high school and my heartfelt prayer of surrender, God opened doors for me to join a vibrant church youth group. My first time attending I learned about the ministry of the Holy Spirit, which changed everything. In the beginning of the Bible, the very first verses in the very first chapter in the very first book, we read of the Spirit being an integral part of creation. "In the beginning, God created the heavens and the earth. The earth was without form and void, and darkness was over the face of the deep. And the Spirit of God was hovering over the face of the waters" (Genesis 1:1–2, ESV).

I learned some of His names: Comforter, Healer, Counselor, Teacher, Helper.

I learned that Jesus said it was to our advantage for Him to leave and go to heaven because then He would send the Spirit to all of us (John 16:7).

I learned that the Spirit gives us power to be witnesses for Jesus (Acts 1:8).

I learned that the fruit of the Spirit is love, joy, peace, patience, kindness, goodness, faithfulness, gentleness, and self-control (Galatians 5:22–23).

I learned that He doesn't enter and possess people like some strange ghost or take over like an alien, using the human body as a host. He has personhood in that He has attributes of intellect, will, emotion, and agency—the ability to act apart from us.

I learned that the Holy Spirit is the one who convicts us of sin, the one who guides us into all truth because He is the Spirit of truth, the one who exists to bear witness to and glorify the Son. The Holy Spirit is God, part of the Trinity, and the same power that raised Jesus from the dead is available to you and me through His indwelling.

Not everyone learns about the importance of relying on God's Spirit early in her Christian life. In fact, the message of too many sermons goes something like this:

God is good.

You are bad.

Try harder.

When convicted of an area that needs transformation, if our first response is "I will do better; I will try harder," then the focus is on doing life in our power. The sooner we realize the futility of self-reliance and the power available to us through the Spirit, the sooner we begin to cooperate with God's purposes and plans and mature into the people He would have us be.

Maturing in Christ

When I think about my kids and their developmental stages, I realize they initially relied on me to provide for all their needs. Over time they learned to walk, then run, then drive. The transition from dependence to independence is a natural part of the maturation process. But often in the Christian life, we find paradox. The last shall be first, and to gain your life you must lose it. Maturity in the Christian life actually looks like *increased* faith and dependence. We begin our relationship with God by faith, we are justified by faith, and then we are filled and empowered through the Holy Spirit by faith. This is what walking by faith is all about.

Maturity requires three components: dependence, obedience, and time. Dependence means our source is God alone. The yielding of our lives and will to Him is what demonstrates a posture of dependence. Obedience is choosing to do the right thing and following God's will and His plan and process. Time is simply time. Weeds grow overnight, but established trees that endure through the seasons of life require time. We need all three components to grow spiritually. The only way we can do this is by replacing self-reliance with God-reliance. This principle continues a theme of this upside-down kingdom where greatness does not come in the form of power, wealth, and popularity but in humble dependence on God.

As I read the Old Testament, I'm struck with how God delivered the Israelites over and over but differently each time. Sometimes He blinded the enemies (2 Kings 6:18) or caused them to hear sounds that created panic and led them to abandon camp (7:6). Sometimes the Israelites battled hand to hand and were overtaken by utter exhaustion, yet still God provided victory (1 Samuel 30:9–25). Sometimes God wiped out the enemy before they arrived (2 Chronicles 20:22–24).

God instructed the Israelites, "Hear, O Israel, you are approaching the battle against your enemies today. Do not be fainthearted. Do not be afraid, or panic, or tremble before them, for the LORD your God is the one who goes with you, to fight for you against your enemies, to save you" (Deuteronomy 20:3–4).

God's people learned over and over to rely on Him rather than on their own wits and wisdom. In the New Testament, too, we see incidents of Jesus healing people with various ailments, and each time is different. Sometimes He simply spoke (John 5:8), sometimes He touched (Matthew 8:3), sometimes He wasn't even nearby but healed from a distance (Mark 7:29–30), and sometimes He spit on their eyes (ew!) (Mark 8:23).

In 1 Chronicles 13:1–4, David, the newly appointed king of Israel, expressed his desire to know and follow God's will. The previous king, Saul, kept disobeying God and taking matters into his own hands. David, in sharp contrast, demonstrated his humble dependence on God and the counsel of others as he contemplated his first decisions as king. Bringing the ark back to Jerusalem landed at the top of his list because the ark represented God's presence to the people of Israel. King David wanted the visual reminder of the ark to highlight the importance of keeping God at the center of all activity and to designate worship as central to God's people. David also showed dependence on God as he consulted Him regarding going to war against the Philistines (1 Chronicles 14:10, 14). As I think about David's life and the description God gave David earlier as being a man after God's own heart (1 Samuel 13:14), I am sobered knowing of his eventual choices to commit adultery and murder. I wonder how his life might have looked had he maintained a posture of dependence on God through inquiring of Him before taking action.

In the book of Galatians, the apostle Paul addressed the believers who went astray and returned to bondage under the law. They sought justification through their own efforts by observing "days and months and seasons and years" instead of through faith in Christ's finished work on the cross (Galatians 4:9–10). Perhaps they were misled because of ignorance, or perhaps "works" provided a false sense of security and control.

In my own life I've realized that the self-reliant approach can actually feel good because it feeds my pride. In my early days as a believer, grace and freedom through Jesus initially felt risky because my faith no longer rested in my controlling ways but in Christ. But when I chose pride, self-sufficiency, and willfulness, the outcome led to living out my faith in my own power, which ultimately did not end well.

True Freedom

Left to ourselves we cannot live in the center of God's will. However, the sweetness of the gospel restores and makes right, adopting us into the lineage of those who are free. True freedom is found in our relationship with Jesus. Paul said it so well in his letter to the Romans:

> There is now no condemnation for those who are in Christ
> Jesus. For the law of the Spirit of life in Christ Jesus has set you
> free from the law of sin and of death. For what the Law could

not do, weak as it was through the flesh, God did: sending His
own Son in the likeness of sinful flesh and as an offering for
sin, He condemned sin in the flesh, so that the requirement of
the Law might be fulfilled in us, who do not walk according to
the flesh but according to the Spirit. (8:1–4)

I have deep respect for Alcoholics Anonymous (AA) and the
Twelve Steps program. Decade after decade lives are saved as women
and men who previously lived trapped in a lonely cycle of destruction
finally get honest and humble. Many first hit rock bottom, and from
this place of brokenness, they surrender and admit their need for a
higher power. The founders of the AA program drew the basis of the
twelve steps from the book of James. The first three steps can be sum-
marized in an easy-to-remember fashion:

1. I can't.
2. God can.
3. Let Him.

Surrender transforms.

And surrender isn't about having a more compliant personality or
preference for following rather than leading. Surrender has to do with
the posture of our hearts.

I remember spending a summer with my friend Helen during college. I admired everything about her. She enjoyed an intimate relationship with God and possessed spiritual depth, maturity, and knowledge
of the Bible. We met together to pray for our friends on missions trips
around the world and to encourage each other in our Bible-reading
plans.

One time in particular I remember sitting cross-legged on a large boulder next to a babbling stream, our Bibles open, the birds chirping, and the sky a vibrant Colorado blue—a truly Pinterest-worthy scene. We closed our eyes to pray, and I happened to open my eyes just as an ugly creepy-crawly bug scurried across the pages of my Bible. I lifted my hand, ready to smash bug guts everywhere. In that second Helen cupped her hands and let the insect crawl on board. She carefully released the bug in the nearby grass.

Helen's deep-brown eyes matched her voice, kind and steady. She embodied gentleness—reserved, quiet, shy, soft spoken, introverted. When friends sought her out for counsel, her doe-like eyes would close slowly as her head tilted in a slow nod of understanding. Kind to all God's creation, she did not squish bugs. Helen embodied everything I was not.

Back then I equated gentle with shy. Verses such as 1 Peter 3:4, "Let your adorning be the hidden person of the heart with the imperishable beauty of a gentle and quiet spirit, which in God's sight is very precious" (ESV), left me desperately wondering how to willfully become shy. Further study on the word *gentle,* however, yielded both unexpected relief and challenge. The Greek word for "gentleness," *praotēs,* is defined as meekness, which means "strength under control."[3] The image is one of a beautiful, strong stallion trained under bit and bridle. The stallion retains all his tremendous strength but now operates under the control of a master. So, too, we retain our personality, gifts, and strengths when we enter into relationship with God. Through the Holy Spirit we are empowered to submit our strength to the greater strength and kingdom purposes of our God.

Gentleness is not weakness; it is not a personality bent, a sentimental softness, or a passively quite manner. It is a fruit of the Spirit

(Galatians 5:22–23) that enables a believer to place the will of God before his own. I still think of Helen as one of the gentlest people I've ever known, but now I understand that the fruit of gentleness, rather than making us shy, calls us to be *surrendered.*

Regardless of whether our personality is type A or we like serving behind the scenes, we each will wrestle with the issue of who will run the show. Our natural tendency when faced with challenges is either to escape and numb out or to grab for control.

Jesus extends an invitation to us all: "Come to me, all who labor and are heavy laden, and I will give you rest. Take my yoke upon you, and learn from me, for I am gentle and lowly in heart, and you will find rest for your souls. For my yoke is easy, and my burden is light" (Matthew 11:28–30, esv). Note how many times He refers to Himself in these two verses. Jesus, arguably the most selfless person, refers to Himself *six* times and explains the antidote to self-reliance. Jesus invites us to draw near to *Him,* not a philosophy, a vacation, or inactivity; rather, rest is found in Him. The image of the yoke and ox is that of an older ox training a young ox. The experienced ox carries the full weight of the yoke on his shoulders. The young ox needs only to bow his head low, get under the yoke, and walk next to the older ox. Jesus calls to us to humble ourselves and be under His direction and care—to walk where He walks, at the pace He chooses, to the places He selects. In this place of surrender, we find true soul rest. No need to strive, to rush about, and to make things happen.

Each day, sometimes even moment by moment, we have a choice to make regarding our will. Will we surrender our self-reliance and entrust our circumstances to God? Or will we keep clutching and grabbing for control, striving in our own effort, and missing out on deeper intimacy with the One who knows us best and loves us most? Whatever we decide, it will change the course of our lives.

This decision to surrender reflects the posture of our hearts.

Questions for Reflection and Discussion

1. Think of a time when you depended on your own limited strength and resources instead of on God's. Where did this take you?

2. When you slip into self-reliance, what is your go-to default to get things under control? Do you rely on your personal experience or gifts? Business models or ministry strategies? Do you work to do better or try harder?

3. Think of a time when God didn't work the way you expected. What happened, and what did you learn?

4. What is your experience of relying on the Holy Spirit within you? What could you study in regard to the Holy Spirit that might help you connect with Him more?

5. What are your thoughts on the statement "Maturity in the Christian life actually looks like *increased* faith and dependence"? How might this look in your life going forward?

6. Which component of maturity would you like to explore further—dependence, obedience, or time?

7. Have you experienced a time when God didn't seem to be moving fast enough? If so, what did you do?

8. After reading this chapter, what do you think about Dallas Willard's statement "The Christian life is what you do when you realize you can do nothing"? How will you respond in the midst of your particular circumstances?

5

Busyness

In repentance and rest you will be saved, in quietness
and trust is your strength.

—ISAIAH 30:15

Several years ago I found myself flat on my back in our master
bedroom, memorizing the quirky design of the popcorn ceiling.
Multiple surgeries, chemotherapy, and radiation for breast cancer took
my body to lows I had never experienced before. I could no longer
function in ministry or contribute to help our family. I felt guilt and
shame over my lack of productivity. With serving God and others removed from my to-do list, I wrestled with my worth. I knew in my
head that God loved and accepted me apart from my good works, but
I questioned it in my heart.

I learned during that time how important it is to ask ourselves *why*
we do what we do. Are we striving and busy so we can earn brownie
points from God? Do we think we need to get everything just so to
garner God's favor and other people's approval? Are we comparing

ourselves with others and telling ourselves we're coming up short? Is God directing our steps, or do we say yes to every opportunity because we're afraid of disappointing someone if we say no? Sometimes in our zeal, out of sincere love for God and others, we fill our every waking moment without honoring the fact that we have human limitations. In the same way that self-reliance is an obstacle to resting in the center of God's will, trying too hard to "do" for God can lead to disillusionment, even despair, because we run on fumes.

Society prizes the over-the-top schedule as a status symbol. Just glance at the top hits on a Google search about being busy, and articles will pop up like "Why Being Busy Is a Status Symbol in the US," "Americans: Overworked and Overstressed," "Research: Why Are Americans So Impressed by Busyness?" Life is full of harried people with full external lives but bankrupt internal lives. Not only do many of us live at breakneck speed in our work lives, but we can also overload in doing ministry. Those of us in vocational Christian work especially can find ourselves doing God's work for the wrong reasons.

Don't get me wrong; we are designed to do important work for the glory of God. Men and women are to colabor as God's image bearers to rule His creation (Genesis 1:26–28). In other words, part of how God designed us is to express, create, and contribute through meaningful work. From the beginning Eve is described as a "helper" (2:18). The Hebrew word is *ezer,* and it is used twenty-one times in the Old Testament. Sixteen of those times are in relation to God Himself as Israel's strong helper.

It is interesting to note that these instances of *ezer* are used consistently in a military context. God created women to be ezer-warriors along with our brothers. Our roles and activities may change over the course of our lifetimes, but we are ezers from cradle to grave. When I think of the contribution of women throughout time in all spheres and in all places, I am, in a word, proud. In many ways women make the world go round. A Chinese proverb translates, "Women hold up half the sky."

Jesus embraced women and affirmed their dignity, worth, and purpose. He sought out, valued, and honored women through His words, attitude, and actions. Jesus's inclusion of women in both discipleship and ministry broke down gender, social, economic, and spiritual barriers and restored the original picture God had in mind when He created male and female. Jesus understood that His purposes and plans to spread the gospel and make disciples of all the nations (Matthew 28:19–20) included, and would not take place apart from, the involvement and contribution of women. Whereas the culture at the time largely discounted women, Jesus did the opposite. He welcomed women as part of the grand story, not props or stagehands, affirming that women play a vital role in ushering in God's kingdom on earth. Nowhere in Scripture do we find an instance where Jesus belittled, yelled at, shamed, or harassed a woman. He treated women with kindness and respect. He did not shy away from speaking hard truth, but He did so in an honorable way.

Bottom line: Jesus is good to women. And I imagine He is proud, as I am, of the women all over the world today—in some cultures considered property, lacking civil rights, working with limited resources, and having few opportunities for schooling and advancement—who have contributed in spectacular ways against all odds. The resilience and resourcefulness of women is simply awe inspiring. That said, sometimes we risk burning out when we believe, consciously or unconsciously, that we are worthwhile only when we are "doing."

Good Enough

My friend Tricia is amazing. An incredibly gifted leader. A natural people gatherer. On each of her party favors at her wedding, for her more than one hundred guests, she wrote personal notes of appreciation. She is thoughtful, hardworking, fun, and wise. She is loved and admired wherever she goes—a woman of excellence through and through.

When she was expecting her first child, her baby shower rivaled the best Pinterest boards—complete with a tasty spread, fun games, creative decorations, and a beautiful guest book to sign with space for encouraging words. As I sat on the edge of the chair with pen in hand, looking over at beautiful, pregnant Tricia, I wondered, *What words of encouragement can I share on a three-by-three-inch piece of paper for this soon-to-be mom?* Parenting, like marriage, brings up all sorts of unfinished business from our families of origin. In our attempts either to be just like our parents or to fulfill a vow of "when I become a parent, I will never ____," we place all sorts of expectations on ourselves and those around us of how we think life should be. We hope and pray our children will grow up to be loving, forgiving, grateful, responsible, and generous. We anticipate they will play fair, sit by the new kid, resolve conflict, love Jesus, keep a budget, be cavity-free, work hard, play hard, be respectful, and keep their rooms and nails clean. All this while we provide a dusted and orderly home with a well-stocked fridge, vegetable-filled meals, and healthy snacks, including apples that don't brown. Oh, and clean, folded clothes and ironed (what's that?) shirts and matching socks without holes. We are the parents who are affectionate, wise, affirming, fair, patient, and consistent and who still hold hands with our spouses while walking through the parking lot.

Sadly, this picture is difficult to attain for most of us, and for the rare few who do, it is impossible to sustain. Life becomes increasingly complex when kids come along, and more often than not all does not go according to plan. The words I wish I had heard (and maybe I did but just didn't take them in) and the words I need to hear even today are the same ones I wrote to Tricia in her guest book: *You are good enough.* For me, as I tackle parenting, my to-do list, the piles of paperwork, my overflowing email inbox, the sliding glass doors covered with doggy nose prints, and the sticky mess in the meat-and-cheese drawer in the fridge, I can't and won't get to all of it today, tomorrow, or even next year. It's not that I won't work hard and invest time in important things, but there is no end to the things I could or should be doing.

So "good enough" for me means being at peace with

○ life in general being less than perfect

○ my little world being less than perfect

○ me being less than perfect

It means letting go of the expectation that life should look different than it does at any given moment. It means rolling with the circumstances God allows, both pleasant and challenging. It means enjoying the enjoyable and persevering in the difficult. It means giving myself, my husband, my kids, and the other people in my life grace to be in process. I whisper "good enough" to myself throughout the day and reassure myself that I actually can be a good enough mom, wife, friend, and anything else God calls me to be. "Good enough" helps me let go and enjoy the present rather than strive toward the next goal or an elusive state of perfection.

I'm Only Human

The books of Kings read like a Korean soap opera. After Solomon's reign the kingdom split into the northern kingdom of Israel and the southern kingdom of Judah. God sent prophets to each kingdom. To Judah He sent Obadiah, Joel, Isaiah, Micah, Nahum, Zephaniah, Jeremiah, and Habakkuk. To Israel He sent Elijah, Elisha, Amos, and Hosea. In the southern kingdom we see a handful of kings who followed the Lord, but in the northern kingdom nineteen evil kings ruled consecutively in Israel! With this as a backdrop, let's look more closely at the prophet Elijah.

Elijah hails from the village of Tishbe, south of the Sea of Galilee. God calls him to prophesy against two of the wicked kings, Ahab and Ahaziah, and warn them of God's punishment: a drought in the capital city of Samaria. God directs Elijah to hide out by the brook Cherith and commands birds to bring him food (1 Kings 17:3–4). Then God directs Elijah to go to the city of Zarephath to have a poor widow provide for him even though she and her son are starving.

When Elijah arrives, hungry and thirsty, the widow is collecting sticks to prepare a final meal before she and her child die. Elijah has the audacity to ask for food and water first, before the widow and her son eat. The widow balks: "As the LORD *your* God lives, I have no bread, only a handful of flour in the bowl and a little oil in the jar" (verse 12, emphasis mine). The widow recognizes that Elijah is a prophet of God, but this God is not her God. Still, somehow she has enough faith to fulfill the prophet's request. He assures her, "The bowl of flour shall not be exhausted, nor shall the jar of oil be empty, until the day that the LORD sends rain" (verse 14). Trusting that Elijah is telling the truth about what his God will do, the widow prepares the meal and feeds Elijah first. As a result, she and her household eat, and the flour and oil are miraculously replenished just as God promised they would be. This is a story of faith on everyone's part, of following God's will even when it doesn't make sense.

Later the widow's son grows ill and eventually dies. This turn of events is not only devastating in itself, but in the culture at the time, being a widow without a son destined her for a bleak future. Women were considered property and had no legal rights. The only way women could secure their place in society was through marriage and mother-hood. Without a son the widow would likely resort to prostitution or servitude to survive.

The widow has allowed Elijah to stay in an upstairs room in her home. After the son dies, the widow and Elijah are distraught. Elijah prays for God to bring him back to life. God revives the child and re-stores him to his mother (verses 17–24). God is performing miracles right and left!

Then, in the second half of chapter 18, we read about the incred-ible victory Elijah has over the 450 false prophets of Baal. In this un-folding of events, we see Elijah pitted against zealous religious leaders in a showdown to prove whose god is the true God. A huge crowd gathers, and Elijah explains that he's the only prophet of the Lord left. He tells the people, "If the LORD is God, follow Him; but if Baal, fol-low him" (verse 21). To prove which is the real God and the one worth following, Elijah instructs that two oxen be brought as sacrifices. The butchered oxen are to be placed on an altar across wood, and then the rival prophets will each have a turn to ask their deities to burn up the sacrifice. Whichever answers by bringing down fire in acceptance of the offering will prove to be the true God.

Everyone agrees to the terms. Elijah explains that since Baal has so many prophets, they should go first. So they begin calling out to Baal for three hours straight. No answer. Elijah teases, "Maybe your god fell asleep and needs to be awakened!" This infuriates the prophets, who scream louder and cut themselves until they bleed. Finally, after they've spent the entire day trying to bring fire down from heaven, Elijah moves the prophets away and calls the people to come near.

The Lord's altar has been trampled by the frenzied prophets and needs repair. Elijah repairs the altar by himself, then digs a deep trench around it and instructs the people to saturate the offering with water—not once, not twice, but three times. The sacrifice, the wood, and the altar are drenched. Then Elijah fills the trench itself with water and prays for God to show the people He is the true God. Fire immediately consumes the offering, the wood, and the stones and licks up all the water. The people respond by falling on their faces and declaring, "Yahweh, He is God!" This is a massive slam-dunk miracle. Elijah and Yahweh #ftw!

The final miracle in chapter 18 is the welcome relief of rain after three and a half years of drought. Elijah confidently sends his servant seven times up to the highest point overlooking the sea, and finally clouds appear and dump torrential rain (verses 41–45).

Despite God's showing up in so many extraordinary ways, however, in the very next chapter, we see Elijah running for his life from

Queen Jezebel and begging God to let him die (19:1–4)! The queen threatens Elijah and he bolts in fear. What a contrast of behavior— and yet so common among those who experience significant success or spiritual breakthroughs. Elijah is exhausted—physically and spiritually depleted. After having amazing experiences of divine intervention, he seems to contract amnesia. When confronted by threats from the wicked queen, Elijah responds in fear rather than faith. He runs away and hides under a tree, thinking he is the only one left who has stayed true to God. His tank on empty, he falls asleep. When he wakes up, he discovers that an angel has left him food and water. He eats, drinks, and falls asleep a second time.

We can draw at least two principles from Elijah's story:

1. *It's okay to be human.* Twice we see Elijah fall fast asleep, and twice we see the angel ministering to him by providing bread and water (verses 5–8). We should not hold back from tending to our physical needs for rest and sustenance. After any big task or event, we need to take time to replenish ourselves.

Solomon penned these perspective-restoring lines:

Unless the LORD builds the house,
They labor in vain who build it;
Unless the LORD guards the city,
The watchman keeps awake in vain.
It is vain for you to rise up early,
To retire late,
To eat the bread of painful labors;
For He gives to His beloved even in his sleep.
(Psalm 127:1–2)

The choice to rest is foundational to God's design of us and as natural as the rhythm of the seasons. We all need to take time out from perpetual busyness to sharpen the proverbial ax. Neglecting our health, filling our bodies with processed food because we are always out of time and running late, not having time for recreation or hobbies or reading a book for fun, and believing we can't grab time with kindred spirits over a meal or coffee are all signs that we are overextended.

2. *God's will cannot be done in isolation.* Elijah wanted God to take his life not only because he was physically exhausted but also because, in his depleted state, he believed he was all alone. "I have been very zealous for the LORD, the God of hosts; for the sons of Israel have forsaken Your covenant, torn down Your altars and killed Your prophets with the sword. And I alone am left; and they seek my life, to take it away" (1 Kings 19:10). The Enemy uses isolation as his most subversive tactic. We need to pay attention anytime we begin to believe the lie that we are the only ones struggling.

After being strengthened by the food supernaturally provided by the angel, Elijah journeys forty days to Mount Horeb. He finds a cave, and God meets him, asking twice, "What are you doing here, Elijah?" (verses 9, 13). When Elijah complains that he is the last man standing, God instructs him to stay on the mountain as God passes by him. Elijah looks for God but does not find him in the loud, glaring experiences like the wind, earthquake, or fire. Only in a gentle whisper is He revealed (verses 11–13). I wonder if Elijah could finally hear God only after his heart settled and he was at peace. In this place of calm, God instructs Elijah to find Elisha (verse 16). Elisha ministers to Elijah (verse 21), and Elijah prepares Elisha to eventually replace him as

God's prophet. Elijah needed companionship, as do each of us. A just-me-and-Jesus posture will not sustain us for the long haul. We need community.

Rhythms of Rest

God Himself modeled rest when He ceased from work on the seventh day of creation (Genesis 2:2–3). God didn't rest because making the world proved taxing. God exists outside time and space; He merely speaks, and the worlds come into being; He is never hurried or late or tired; His resources are unlimited. And yet He chose to rest.

In Hebrew, two different words are used for "rest." The first word is *shabath,* and it has three meanings. The first is "to stop, cease, or desist." Basically, God stops and takes a break. A second meaning is "to celebrate." God admires His work, then sets aside an entire day to enjoy the fruit of His labor. The third meaning is "to suffer to be lacking," or to tolerate not having everything tied up in a bow. We need to choose rest despite the incompleteness of our situations, trusting that God will provide in the future at the proper time. We can choose to stop and celebrate despite having things undone.

The second word for rest is *menuchah,* which means "a settled home, a place to be, an abode."[4] So we find rest as we find our home in God and draw from our relationship with Him. Sally Breedlove wrote in her book *Choosing Rest,*

> Even before rest became a part of the Law, God wanted His
> people to stop, to celebrate, to trust that tomorrow would work
> out even if they took the breaks He prescribed. He longed for

His people to be at home with Him, to realize they needed
time when relationship, not work, filled their souls.[5]

Looking at Jesus's life and example, we see that He, too, never
rushed and never fretted. He knew when to push through and continue ministering to others and when to pull away to get recharged
and spend time with His Father. He lived in the tension of the masses
still needing healing and His commitment to follow His Father's will.
When I observe Jesus's years of ministry, I don't find a mystifying
work/life/family balance. He had times when He ministered day and
night. Falling so soundly asleep in the middle of such a huge storm
that even seasoned fishermen found terrifying suggests He experienced weary-to-the-bone fatigue (Mark 4:35–41). But contrast this to
other times in Jesus's ministry: He "would often slip away to the wilderness and pray" (Luke 5:16). Jesus's life was full, but not busy.

The bottom line is that a willing heart is a rested heart. A quiet
heart. A heart freed from endless doing. Out of His love and intimate
knowledge of us as His creation, God puts in place rhythms of rest.
His desire for us to stop, celebrate, and trust Him for tomorrow is reflected in the concept of the Sabbath, a time intentionally set apart to
rest and rejuvenate.

Peter Scazzero, in his book *The Emotionally Healthy Leader,*
shared how he looked put together as a senior pastor of a large, growing, multiethnic church in Queens, New York City, but on a personal
level had become a workaholic "for God." He explained that his emotional immaturity negatively affected his home life as a husband and
father.[6] Out of frustration and desperation—and ultimately the grace
of God—his wife, Geri, quit his church. Stopped going altogether.

Her decision propelled him on a journey of self-reflection, and through a skilled therapist he began to understand the unhealthy patterns in his life and the triggers that led to poor choices. He learned to embrace Sabbath as a gift from the Lord.

As a pastor Peter's weekly Sabbath was from 6 p.m. on Friday to 6 p.m. on Saturday. These are the areas he focused on during the time he set aside:

○ *Stop:* He stopped all paid and unpaid work.

○ *Rest:* He replaced work with what he found replenishing: napping, working out, taking long walks, reading a novel, watching a good movie, or going out for dinner. He avoided the computer and his cell phone during his time off from labor. (Can you even imagine not holding a cell phone and scrolling for a whole day?)

○ *Delight:* He took time to notice beauty and pay attention to things that brought him delight, like nature, hiking, the beach, music, travel, and family time.

○ *Contemplate:* Peter recognized that Sabbath is an opportunity to focus on being with Jesus and to acknowledge God in all things. He accepted the invitation to slow down in order to walk closely with Jesus and replenish himself spiritually for the week ahead.[7]

One of my friends who practices the Sabbath well helps her young children understand the concept by lighting a special candle each week when the family's Sabbath time begins. Another friend loves to cook, so during the Sabbath she deliberately slows down and takes her time preparing meals. She chops and stirs unhurried. She tastes the food she prepares and chews slowly, taking time to savor the various flavors. Another friend chooses to stroll instead of walk at her regular frantic pace. Sabbath can include taking time to get away to a coffee shop to read a good book while the baby naps or having some extended time with God by reading the Bible and journaling. As a college student I chose not to study on Sundays. These days I am diligent about setting aside a full twenty-four hours for Sabbath rest. I light a special candle to help remind my family and me when the time begins and ends. I try to walk slower, drive slower, breathe slower, chew slower, and relish every moment.

I encourage you to take a step toward practicing the Sabbath or some form of rest on a weekly basis. See for yourself how this discipline helps you live more purposefully and joyfully. Few other things can move our hearts toward living out God's will day to day.

Our First Love

The founder of Cru, Dr. Bill Bright, when asked if he had any prayer requests, would most frequently answer, "Pray I won't lose my first love." He didn't ask for more donations or greater ministry influence; his simple request was that he would keep his heart aligned with the Father's. His aspiration can help us evaluate the condition of our own hearts.

In Revelation 2:2–4 Jesus said to the church in Ephesus, one of the leading spiritual centers of the time, "I know your deeds and your toil and perseverance, and that you cannot tolerate evil men, and you put to the test those who call themselves apostles, and they are not, and you found them to be false; and you have perseverance and have endured for My name's sake, and have not grown weary. But I have this against you, that you have left your first love."

The church in Ephesus focused on very important work. They toiled and demonstrated dedication to righting wrongs and sticking it out despite hard circumstances. God acknowledged this. But He called them out on the fact that they were overlooking the essentials of their faith as they filled their lives with "good" activities. They were missing God in the process.

As one who easily can be swept into the current of doing things *for* God and is often in the presence of gifted women leaders, I find myself praying frequently that loving to do things for God doesn't replace loving God. I pray we will tend our souls well so no obstacles prevent the outflowing of His love to the world around us.

John Ortberg, in his book *Soul Keeping,* told the story of a town high in the Alps and an old man who served as Keeper of the Springs. His work, removing debris that could pollute the water, happened behind the scenes. The town council decided to reallocate the money used to hire the old man, so he left his post. At first no one noticed, but after a while the stream grew brackish and the people in the village fell ill. The life of the village depended on the stream, and the life of the stream depended on the keeper. The city council rehired the old man, and the villagers were restored to health. Ortberg explained, "The stream is your soul. And you are the keeper."[8]

We may experience God's deliverance and take part in great spiritual victories. We may see growth in our various ministries and numbers of lives being changed for the better. But if we miss the Lord in the midst of doing even good and honorable activities for Him, then we miss everything. May you and I make spending quality time with Jesus and loved ones a high priority, drawing close to the One who can clear the debris and guard our souls.

 Questions for Reflection and Discussion

1. Spend some time carefully considering how many hours of
   your week are focused on "doing" rather than "being." What
   stands out or surprises you?

2. Is it hard for you to rest? If you feel you are too busy, why is
   that so?

3. Think of a time when you said yes to something because you
   were afraid to say no. What can you do differently next time
   to have more integrity and take care of yourself?

4. Have you ever been guilty of doing God's work for the
   wrong reasons? In what way?

5. What does being "good enough" mean to you? What might
   you let go of if you thought you were good enough without it?

6. Have you experienced a letdown or sense of defeat following
   a significant success or spiritual breakthrough? What
   happened? What helped you move forward?

7. In what ways have you been neglecting your body, soul, or relationships? What can you do to change this?

8. How can you set aside some form of Sabbath in your life? Which of the four areas identified by Peter Scazzero could you integrate more fully: stop, rest, delight, or contemplate?

6

Bitterness

Be kind to one another, tender-hearted, forgiving each
other, just as God in Christ also has forgiven you.

—EPHESIANS 4:32

The picture, drawn in black ballpoint pen on the back of a junk-mail envelope, looked straightforward. My aunt, a talented artist who painted intricate watercolor peonies and Chinese scenery on scrolls, managed to convince me to let her cut off some of my long hair to help me stay cooler in the heat of a Colorado summer. I was nine years old and my thick, straight jet-black hair grew long past my waist. My aunt's simple, quickly drawn sketch depicted my hair falling around the middle of my back with a nice curve at the ends, shaped like a smile. With a twinkle in her eye, she tapped the envelope with her pen, smiled, and said to me in Chinese, "There. Something like this. It will make you more comfortable to not have so much hair weighing you down." I held the envelope and studied the picture.

Halfway down my back seemed reasonable, so I agreed, and we began to assemble a home salon in the bathroom.

My aunt placed a chair inside the bathtub, and I sat down with a towel draped around my shoulders. After combing through my wet hair that fell past the edge of the chair, she took a pair of silver fabric scissors and grasped a handful of my damp hair in her hand. The metal blades sliced through my hair. Above my right ear. Nearly two feet of hair fell around my bare feet.

I froze. My aunt finished cutting and left me sitting in the bathtub. Mustering up all my courage, I stood up and turned to look in the mirror. I looked like a boy.

I slumped into a ball and began wailing. I cried alone in the bathroom until my tears ran out. Exhausted, I pulled myself together but shut my aunt out of my heart.

For nearly ten years I conveniently "forgot" the incident ever happened. As a textbook conflict avoider, I have mastered "Oh, it's okay" when in truth whatever "it" is, is *not* okay. But during my freshman year of college, I was sitting on the edge of my bed staring at a blank sheet of paper. In Bible study we were studying forgiveness, and our homework was simple: ask God to show us anything we needed to be forgiven for and anything we needed to forgive. We were to write these out, bring each before God, and then rip up or burn the paper. I wondered what the Holy Spirit would reveal.

Surprisingly, an incident in the sixth grade when stickpins were all the rage came to mind. The girls went crazy over these enormous three-inch pins with little designs on the end. The stickpins, worn outside sweaters and shirts, had a cover for their sharp point. I'm absolutely sure these pins would top the list of items banned from school today. Who lets elementary-age kids bring big, sharp pins to school? Well, stickpins back then, along with jumbo Bonne Bell Lip Smackers, were the equivalent of today's fidget spinners and slime. When I lost the piece of my pin that protected its sharp tip, I couldn't wear it any longer, so during a trip to the local Kmart, I stole the missing piece from one of the stickpins on display. Since God had brought my theft to mind, I wrote it down on the top line of my paper.

Then, completely out of the blue, the hair-cutting incident came flooding back, along with an unexpected torrent of emotions. Tears burned in my eyes as I recalled what happened. I realized at that moment why I left the room whenever my aunt entered and why I didn't look her in the eyes and remained guarded and cool toward her. I stopped wishing her well, and compassion and concern for her dissolved. I actually felt glad when I heard of any misfortunes or difficulties in her life.

As I remembered and wrestled, I considered that what she did certainly warranted my distrust. She lied. She never admitted her wrongdoing or apologized. And all the excuses I told myself—"Oh, it's just hair; it will grow back" or "She probably didn't realize what she did was wrong; after all, she'd recently moved from another country and probably felt confused"—suddenly felt hollow. The tears spilling down my cheeks were evidence of the hurt and betrayal I still felt.

But God's Spirit clearly directed me to forgive my aunt. He knew my buried pain and resentment were only keeping the hurt alive. It's been said, "Unforgiveness is like drinking poison and waiting for the other person to die." I took up my pen and paper and chose to forgive:

I forgive my aunt for lying to me when I was a little girl, for betraying me and taking advantage of my helplessness and compliance, and for cutting off all my hair.

I didn't expect to experience what came next. After writing out the rest of my "sin list," shredding it, and burning it in the fireplace, I felt lighter. A weight I didn't know I'd been carrying was lifted. While this may not be everyone's experience, as every situation is different, I knew I'd done my part of letting go of the hurt and forgiving as God had asked. The next time I saw my aunt, I experienced evidence of God's supernatural work in my heart. I felt love and affection for her and looked her in the eyes.

It's important to note that relationships sometimes don't heal. Restoration is a two-way street, and trust is earned. But when God instructs us to forgive, it is for our good and not based on the offender's worthiness. Forgiveness is not a decision based on feelings. It's agreeing to live with the consequences of another person's sin and choosing not to harbor resentment or retaliate. We live with those consequences regardless, in either bitterness or freedom. My aunt probably had no recollection of the incident, but I spent years living in bondage to unnamed bitterness.

Forgiveness Liberates

As we go along in life, we often experience circumstances and situations outside our control. We are wronged by others, and we wrong others over and over. The capacity to forgive and be forgiven is a gift from God that enables us to open our hands and release resentments and guilt.

It shouldn't surprise us, but science backs up what God has been saying all along. He knows what we need because He created us, and He knows how we operate best. When it comes to the topic of health, God has instructed us on everything from the importance of physical rest to our need to practice forgiveness in order to live as whole, healthy people. You need only to google "connection between forgiveness and health" to find a plethora of articles written by researchers at Johns Hopkins University and the Mayo Clinic, among other reputable sources, and to see the kindness of the Lord. We experience our fullest lives when we live according to our Creator's example and His ways. But living this way doesn't usually come easily.

In Genesis we read about the miracle of forgiveness in Joseph's life. Cruelly sold into slavery by his jealous brothers (chapter 37), he spends time in prison for doing the right thing by refusing the ongoing invitation from his master's wife and not sleeping with her (chapter 39). Nevertheless, throughout Joseph's story we read how the Lord never leaves him.

During Joseph's time in prison, God gives him the ability to interpret dreams. After correctly explaining the meaning of dreams to both a cupbearer and a baker, he is still forgotten and remains in his cell. Two years pass, and Pharaoh begins having troubling dreams. Finally Joseph is remembered as one who can interpret dreams. He is brought before Pharaoh and correctly describes the dreams and the meaning regarding a future drought in the land. Joseph is released from prison and eventually is promoted to second in command in Egypt (chapter 41).

In God's economy nothing is wasted. Joseph learns through hardship about God's character, and through the trials he learns both humility and perspective on God's ways and God's heart.

When famine takes over the land, Joseph is reunited with his family (chapters 42–45). In the last chapter of Genesis, Joseph explains to his brothers that they do not need to be afraid that he will seek retribution for their behavior toward him: "As for you, you meant evil against me, but God meant it for good in order to bring about this present result, to preserve many people alive" (50:20). God actually allowed all the hardships in Joseph's life, and through one man who was faithful to Him, He saved the populace of an entire region, including God's chosen people, from dying. Joseph's decision to forgive his family came long before they arrived on the scene.

Forgiveness helps us recognize God's presence and hand over our lives despite sometimes horrendous conditions. During World War II Corrie ten Boom's family risked their lives by hiding Jewish families in their home to protect them while Nazis rounded up entire families and sent more than six million Jews to their deaths. When discovered, the ten Boom family also ended up imprisoned in Nazi concentration camps.

After the war God led Corrie to return to Germany with a message that God forgives. Her belief in God's ultimate justice and her need to forgive moved from head to heart the day she came face to face with her greatest challenge. In 1947, in a church basement in defeated Munich, Germany, Corrie finished speaking to a German audience about God's love and forgiveness. As people began filing out, she saw a familiar heavyset man approaching her. A flashback to Ravensbrück made the connection. She remembered this man as one of the harshest soldiers in Ravensbrück, where Corrie and her sister, Betsie, endured unspeakable mistreatment.

With hand outstretched, the man spoke words of appreciation for

Corrie's message. He shared how he had been a guard in the camp Corrie mentioned in her talk. He didn't remember her or Betsie among the thousands of women but explained how he found the Lord after the horrific war. "I know God has forgiven me for the cruel things I did in the camp, but I would like to hear it from your lips as well, Fräulein—will you forgive me?"

Corrie wrestled back and forth as she recalled the horrors she and her sister had endured and the humiliation of being forced to walk naked past this cruel guard. Betsie had died a slow, terrible death in that dreadful place. Could all this be wiped away simply by his asking for forgiveness?

But ultimately Corrie knew she had to forgive—not only based on God's commandment but also based on her personal experience. In the home she ran for victims of Nazi brutality in Holland, she saw firsthand how those who forgave their enemies rebuilt their lives despite their physical or emotional scars. Those who remained bitter remained imprisoned, unable to move forward despite becoming physically free.

Though her heart felt cold, Corrie knew forgiveness was not an emotion but an act of the will. She knew her will could function regardless of the state of her heart in that moment. She prayed for God's help: *I can lift my hand. I can do that much. You supply the feeling.* The way she explained how God answered her feeble prayer is breathtaking:

And so woodenly, mechanically, I thrust my hand into the one stretched out to me. And as I did, an incredible thing took place. The current started in my shoulder, raced down my arm, sprang into our joined hands. And then this healing warmth seemed to flood my whole being, bringing tears to my eyes.

"I forgive you, brother!" I cried. "With all my heart."

For a long moment we grasped each other's hands, the former guard and the former prisoner. I had never known God's love so intensely as I did then."[9]

God knows what we need to live and walk in freedom. He demonstrated and modeled the forgiveness He asks of us as He hung in agony on the cross. "Father, forgive them, for they know not what they do," He pleaded (Luke 23:34, ESV). He not only lives out His own command but also supplies His Spirit to help us do what we cannot without His help.

Forgiveness Restores

Not long ago I lived in my car. At least it seemed that way. I had three kids in three schools. Different activities and schedules had me backing in and out of the driveway constantly. On a random Monday I counted sixteen times.

One day I had just pulled into the garage when Jonathan, my oldest, started sharing about some of his struggles with school and life. Jonathan was in eighth grade at the time, and I knew these windows of heart-to-heart discussion didn't open every day. I gladly remained motionless to continue the conversation. So we sat inside the car in the garage, and Jonathan wondered out loud if the schoolwork and late nights would prove worthwhile. He wondered about his ultimate purpose in life. He processed about God's will and the future. I sat and listened, offered a little perspective, and asked questions. At one point, though I am embarrassed to admit it, I started thinking, *Hey, take this in. We are sitting here talking about some meaningful stuff. Real life—character-focused, developmental stuff. Definitely winning in the mom department here. Secret high five, fist bump, and shoulder pat, Momma. If you were a football player, I'd give your behind a "way to go" slap.*

And then my cell phone rang. I looked at the caller ID. The school office. I picked up and heard my preschooler, Julia, on the other end.

"Mommy, you forgot me."

I looked at the time. Yikes! I'd totally lost track because of the conversation with Jonathan.

"Oh, sweetheart! I'm so sorry. I'll be right over!"

Jonathan got out of the car, and I backed out of the driveway and headed straight to my daughter's school. Julia got into the back seat of the car and sat stone faced and silent. We headed over to pick up her elementary-age brother, Michael, and his friend, Elias. While we waited for them in the pickup line, I asked, "How are you doing, Julia?"

Angry silence.

"I'm so sorry I forgot to pick you up. I was talking with Jonathan and totally lost track of the time."

Icy silence. Arms crossed. Furrowed brow.

She finally asked, "Did you ever forget to pick up either of my brothers?"

"Oh, yes. I'm sure I forgot to pick them up along the way."

Inside I thought, *Are you kidding me? One time. I've dropped you off and picked you up hundreds, maybe thousands, of times without forgetting. One teeny, tiny time and you are not letting me off the hook?*

"Really? How many times did you forget to pick them up?"

"Oh, I can't remember exactly how many. Look, I'm sorry. Will you forgive me?"

No answer.

Inside my thoughts raced. *Really? I had to walk to school. And I grew up in Colorado. And it snowed there. Yeah, I walked to school and back . . . In. The. Snow! And it's not like I was late because I watch soap operas; I was deep in meaningful conversation with your brother. You should be grateful you have a brother. You should be grateful I drive you at all. You should be grateful we even have a car!*

Michael and Elias raced out to the car and tumbled into the back seat full of jokes and high energy, relieved to be released from having to sit still at their desks hour after hour. We returned home and pulled into the garage. The boys headed straight to the fridge, ready to heat up Bagel Bites and find out who could eat a whole tray the fastest.

Back in the garage Julia remained in her seat, unmoving. Thankfully, I listened to the prompting of the Spirit. I got out of the front seat and knelt down by her open door.

"Julia, I wonder if maybe you felt worried when you didn't see me at the pickup line after school. Or maybe you felt scared something had happened to me."

She looked at me and uncrossed her arms. I continued, "And then when all your friends were gone and you had to go wait in the office, I wonder if you felt embarrassed or angry because all the other moms and dads came to pick up their kids and you were the only one left."

She nodded as tears formed in her eyes.

With tears filling my own, I clasped both her hands in mine and looked into her eyes.

"Oh, Julia, you know how sometimes I raise my voice and yell about something, and I have to apologize later because my words were spoken in a way that hurt you? In those times I know that what I did hurt you. But sometimes things I do hurt you that I didn't mean to do, but they still hurt you. Today, when I forgot to pick you up, my actions hurt you. You probably felt all sorts of things—worried, scared, embarrassed, and angry. I am truly sorry."

Julia threw both her arms around my neck and spoke right into my ear, "I forgive you, Mommy."

My little girl needed to be validated in how she felt, and I needed to own my wrong attitude and behavior. Only in this way could our relationship be restored.

In the same way God is always seeking restored relationship with us, so He makes a way. In the Old Testament He set up a complex system involving animal sacrifices to address our sin problem. These sacrifices took place year after year (Hebrews 10:1–4) because people needed to be forgiven over and over. Through Jesus, God made it possible for people to be forgiven once and for all. In Colossians 2:13–14 Paul explained,

When you were dead in your transgressions and the uncircumcision of your flesh, He made you alive together with Him, having forgiven us all our transgressions, having canceled out the certificate of debt consisting of decrees against us, which was hostile to us; and He has taken it out of the way, having nailed it to the cross.

The Greek word for "paid in full" is *tetelestai*. The last utterance Jesus spoke before He died on the cross, "It is finished!" is also *tetelestai*. Jesus took the certificates of debt of all people, of all time, listing *all* our sin, which required the punishment of death, and nailed them to the cross, declaring *tetelestai*, "Paid in full!"

Our sins are forgiven. All of them. Past, present, and future. This truth still takes my breath away. "There is therefore now no condemnation for those who are in Christ Jesus" (Romans 8:1, ESV). Our standing with God is secure and unchanging. It's not a yo-yo, on-again, off-again relationship depending on when (not if) we sin. We don't confess so we can be forgiven; we are forgiven because Jesus paid the penalty for our sin. Jesus's shed blood on the cross, His death, burial, and resurrection have made it possible for us to be declared completely righteous and justified (Romans 3–5). Because of our position in Christ, God sees us as holy and blameless (Colossians 1:22).

That said, this side of heaven we live in tension. We live in the now and the not yet. The other side of justification is a process called sanctification, or being set apart and becoming more like Jesus (2 Corinthians 3:18). This type of spiritual growth lasts all our days. We never fully arrive until we see Jesus face to face. In fact, it's been said, "The closer you walk to the Light, the more dirt you see." This is true in the life of Paul, who authored a big chunk of the New Testament. In his previous life before Jesus appeared to him, he lived as a zealous and devout religious leader (Acts 9). He hated and persecuted Christians, calling for their imprisonment and death. As you read his writings, over the course of time he referred to himself initially as a sinner, but by the end of his life, he referred to himself as a sinner "among whom

I am foremost of all" (1 Timothy 1:15–16). Though Paul admitted to overtly sinful behaviors, over time God's Spirit exposed deeper levels of his sin nature, which drove him to even greater appreciation for his Lord and Savior.

So on one hand, over time God matures us and helps us see how we can live more like Christ; but at the same time He faithfully removes the idols in our hearts we're not even aware of. God's faithfulness to grow us in every way until we are enjoying His presence in heaven is a process that continues all our lives. As we remain on the paths He lays out for us, He will faithfully expose areas in our lives that need His grace and forgiveness. As we realize ever more deeply our need for Christ, we honor Jesus's great sacrifice to reconnect us with the Father and restore us to one another.

Forgiveness Heals

Sometimes we are hardest on ourselves and continue to kick ourselves for mistakes we've made. Learning to forgive myself has brought about healing I didn't even know I needed.

Much of this has come in the form of being restored in the context of community. I remember in college hearing of a string of moral failures on the part of several Christian leaders. Their disqualification from ministry and the implications in their marriages and families, not to mention their churches and organizations, disturbed me deeply. In every one of these situations, each leader displayed a pattern of living and leading in isolation.

I realized no one is immune from committing sexual sin. Often the lure of sin is a way of medicating pain, disappointment, and fear. I've made a commitment not to live my faith in isolation and not to keep secrets. I've sought out safe people with whom I can share openly about my struggles, past and present. I remember confessing and sharing with my best friend at the time all my moral failures. Having her listen and know my past brought about an even deeper healing than I experienced through privately confessing to God.

"Confess your sins to one another, and pray for one another so that you may be healed," James wrote. "The effective prayer of a righteous man can accomplish much" (5:16). In the same way the Nazi guard needed verbal forgiveness from Corrie ten Boom, we, too, are able to experience restoration as we allow others to witness our sin and declare us forgiven. When we bring the truth out into the light, our souls flourish and our lives give glory to God.

Finally, it's important to acknowledge any anger we have toward God. I wonder if Esther struggled with thoughts against God due to losing her parents or being rounded up with other girls like cattle to be paraded for the king's pleasure. Certainly being forced to give her body to a stranger could lead to false thinking about God. We technically don't forgive God since He is perfect, but it's important to renounce false thinking about His character and release any resentment we have toward Him.

In the next portion of the book, we will look more closely at openhanded living and what it means on a practical level. Our willing hearts, now moldable by our heavenly Father, will continue to come up against obstacles, but a beautiful transformation comes when we live with our hearts and lives yielded to the King.

Questions for Reflection and Discussion

1. Have you ever said "Oh, it's okay" to something that was *not* okay and then resented it? What were the consequences?

2. Think of someone you know who has been eaten up by bitterness. What does this look like, and how has it played out?

3. Reflect on this statement: "When God instructs us to forgive, it is for our good and not based on the offender's worthiness. Forgiveness is not a decision based on feelings. It's agreeing to live with the consequences of another person's sin and choosing not to harbor resentment or retaliate." When have you been able to forgive in this way? When have you not?

4. Has there been a situation in your life, like Joseph's, through which God accomplished something good in spite of another's harmful act? If so, how might this help you handle an unhealed hurt or betrayal now?

5. Think of a time when validating another's hurt feelings helped mend your relationship with her. If you have harmed

someone but not owned it, what can you do to help restore your relationship?

6. What do you think of the statement "The closer you walk to the Light, the more dirt you see"? How can Jesus's sacrifice for you help you deal with what you see?

7. Has there been a time when another person has helped you forgive yourself for your failures? If so, how did this feel? How can you be such a person for others?

8. Ask God to show you anything you need to be forgiven for and anything you need to forgive. Ask Him to do what you cannot do without His help. Write out what you hear, bring each of these things before God, and then rip up or burn the paper. What feelings did you have as you moved through this process?

PART 3

LIVING AN OPEN-HANDED LIFE

7

Accepting No

When a train goes through a tunnel and it gets dark,
you don't throw away the ticket and jump off. You sit
still and trust the engineer.

—CORRIE TEN BOOM

If ever we needed prayer, it is now. The pain is indescribable." I read
and reread Maegan's post on Facebook in shock and disbelief. *No!*
There must have been a mistake. This couldn't be. None of the thousands of people from coast to coast and around the world who rallied
in prayer the past several weeks expected the story to end this way.

Three weeks earlier, a motorcycle accident in Arkansas had sent
twenty-year-old Josiah Robins to the emergency room. After realizing
the extent of his injuries, the doctors had him airlifted to Tulsa, Oklahoma. He was in the ICU for weeks. Maegan, his mom, slept on a
chair next to his bed and updated us all on his progress. Everyone
prayed in faith, asking and believing God for complete healing and

restoration. Josiah made steady progress in spite of having both legs amputated. Everything seemed to point to answered prayer.

Then a stroke.

Then he was gone.

God said no.

Two words I most associated with Josiah were *kind* and *grounded*. His quiet strength and the love of his extended family influenced people all over the country. Sorrow flowed through the aisles of a packed church as we gathered to honor and remember this young man of outstanding character.

I've struggled over the outcome of how I thought Josiah's story would end. I've turned over a thousand times in my mind the way his life abruptly came to a close, and I can't make sense of it. Josiah's death wasn't the result of gang violence or alcohol or drugs. His future brimmed with possibilities. As a young African American man, son to a single mom, big brother to his three younger siblings, Josiah lived in stark contrast to poor choices he could have made but didn't. Instead, he leaned into God and with fierce loyalty purposed to love and protect his family. He chose to live in a way that made them proud.

I don't understand.

From Legions to Peace

When I face bewilderment, inevitably I scour the pages of my Bible. More than looking for answers, my eyes search for the Lord.

In Mark 5:1–20 we read about Jesus and the Gerasene man who was possessed by a legion of demons. The demons tormented the man day and night, causing him to cry out and gash himself with stones. The situation became so volatile that he had to be bound by shackles and chains. At some point the chains could no longer hold him; no one was strong enough to subdue him. He was banished to live by himself among the tombs in the mountains. Only his distant screams reminded the villagers of his existence.

Then he saw Jesus from a distance and approached Him. Now, whether or not the man knew who Jesus was, the demons certainly did. They asked Him, "What business do we have with each other, Jesus, Son of the Most High God?" (verse 7).

In several other instances in the Gospels when Jesus approached a person tormented by demons, the demons recognized Him immediately and declared Him to be the Son of the Most High God. James wrote, "You believe that God is one. You do well; the demons also believe, and shudder" (2:19). The demons know and believe that Jesus is exactly who He claims to be. Jesus is not a great philosopher or teacher; He is the way, the truth, and the life. No one comes to the Father but through Him (John 14:6).

Jesus confronted the demons and demanded that they identify themselves. They told Him they were Legion, which is around five thousand strong. They knew they were in trouble in the presence of the Son of the Most High God, so they asked—they *implored*—Jesus to send them into the pigs (Mark 5:12–13).

He said yes.

The herdsmen watched in horror as two thousand swine rushed down a bank into the sea. They returned to the town to report what they saw.

The townspeople arrived and saw the formerly demon-possessed man clothed and in his right mind. This was an incredible, undisputed miracle! A precious life had been restored. I wonder if Jesus healed the man's scars from the gashes he'd inflicted or if they remained as a reminder of what he'd been through. I wonder if one of the disciples took water and a cloth and helped wipe away the dirt and dried blood from the man's face and arms. I wonder how the man felt to be delivered from his suffering and to sit calmly, in total peace. I picture Jesus hugging the man and smiling as He introduced him to the disciples. I wonder about the conversations they shared.

Meanwhile the townspeople got scared. Maybe they thought Jesus would be bad for business, casting more demons into more livestock. Or perhaps they had the same response Peter did when, after bringing in a miraculously huge haul of fish, he realized Jesus was God. Peter fell at Jesus's feet and said, "Depart from me, for I am a sinful man, O Lord" (Luke 5:8, ESV). Whatever the townspeople were afraid of, it caused them to ask—to *implore*—Jesus to leave because they were afraid (Mark 5:17).

He said yes.

What kind of belief do you and I have in Jesus? Mere assent to facts doesn't translate to a life that looks any different from someone who does not believe. The belief John wrote about that leads to saving faith is found in John 1:12: "As many as received Him, to them He gave the right to become children of God, even to those who *believe* in His name" (emphasis mine). In the original Greek, belief is not a passive acceptance of a truth but an active faith demonstrated through the way we live.

A modern-day example is bringing to a pharmacist a piece of paper that a physician with notoriously unintelligible penmanship has scribbled on. The pharmacist then deciphers the words and walks to and fro through rows and rows of pills. She locates some pills and fills a plastic bottle, adheres instructions, and staples the bag holding the bottle. We exercise an active belief and trust in the doctor and the pharmacist when we open the bottle and swallow the pills.

When we believe in Jesus, it is more than just an intellectual understanding that He is the Son of God, and it is more than an emotional experience. It is an exercise of our will, which results in a change in both our thinking and actions. This leaves me evaluating where I operate out of fear in my own life and where I keep Jesus at arm's length. Do I welcome only a safe, tame, comfort-granting Jesus, or do I trust Him in *all* His power and majesty?

The man Jesus gladly delivered from the demons, the man who had been tormented and ostracized, asked—he *implored*—Jesus for permission to accompany Him in the boat to be with Him and the disciples (Mark 5:18).

Jesus said no.

Jesus loved the man He rescued and restored, yet He denied the man's request. I don't know about you, but I want to hear a resounding yes when I make requests of God.

I remember watching the movie *Bruce Almighty,* in which God grants the main character, Bruce, the ability to be God for a time. One of his new responsibilities is to answer every prayer. Bruce starts evaluating each request and after a while becomes so overwhelmed that he issues a universal yes to all prayer requests. Chaos results. If you're a parent, you understand that if you responded to every food request from your young ones with a yes, they would eat cotton candy for breakfast, lunch, and dinner. We have good reason to say no. Why would we think that God doesn't? But still, from our limited viewpoint, we wonder.

As we think back to Esther's situation, Scripture doesn't tell us when, how, or why her parents died. I wonder if she was old enough to know of her parents' predicament. Did she pray and ask Yahweh to spare their lives? If she was old enough to understand the situation, then she experienced what all of us do sooner or later when we make entreaties of God: the hard-to-accept, hard-to-stomach, seemingly unfair response of no. Sometimes the marriage ends; sometimes healing never comes for the child with brain cancer; sometimes the addict returns to his destructive ways; sometimes the incredible, godly, wonderful, wants-to-get-married friend remains single; sometimes the family member doesn't surrender to Christ before she dies; sometimes homes flood beyond repair; sometimes dreams die; sometimes churches have to close their doors; sometimes relationships remain irreconcilable; sometimes we don't get the happily-ever-after life we wanted and prayed for; sometimes wrongs don't get righted. Life isn't fair, and people don't always get what they deserve.

But when God says no to our requests, He never stops loving us. His no doesn't come with His back turned to us in rejection. He takes no pleasure in our pain. The reason Jesus came and died was for the purpose of our restoration.

Grief Heals

Not all pain is the same. Sometimes our circumstances become so difficult that our typical coping methods fail us and we are faced with the true condition of our souls and the necessity of grieving our losses and disappointments.

In their book *How People Grow,* Drs. Henry Cloud and John Townsend described grief as a voluntary pain we enter into. They wrote, *"Grief is the one [pain] that heals all the others. It is the most important pain there is.* This is why God calls us to enter into it voluntarily. It heals. It restores. It changes things that have gone bad. Moreover, *it is the only place where we get comforted when things have gone wrong."*[10]

Besides the deaths of loved ones, some of the things we grieve include difficult seasons of life, broken relationships, financial upheaval, illness, and the death of plans or dreams—basically the loss of anything we wanted or needed. We initially protest through anger or numbing and then move into a state of depression as we let the loss sink in. If we're willing to keep moving, eventually we enter a place of acceptance that our circumstances are not the way we hoped. Sadness fades, and we become available once again for new things.

Josiah's aunt, my friend Kierstin, shared at his memorial service, "Josiah's death is *not* the end of the story." And while I believe Kierstin's words to be true, my heart grieves deeply along with Josiah's family and friends. We feel the sorrow of all Josiah's missed milestones: his college graduation, awards, travels, birthdays, wedding, children. But I hold both grief and hope in tension; I can't help but think that God's no to our prayers for Josiah involves so much more than we know at this point.

Our pain can be redemptive when we stop trying to control or play judge or take on any other role that actually belongs to God. When we surrender to His will and rule in our lives, He promises to use our trials to transform us into His image.

A Reason to Hope

Living with open hands and willing hearts will take us down some painful roads. This is simply part of life. But it is not a reason to give up hope or stop engaging. One of the unexpected by-products of embracing a no from God is how He uses our pain and disappointment to make us stronger and enhance who we truly are in Christ. Like sore muscles after a workout (or so I've heard, since I'm not a real fitness enthusiast), the breakdown and rebuilding are what make the muscles grow stronger and larger. Suffering can take us to places that a life of comfort cannot.

Embracing God's no may be one of the greatest challenges we face as believers. I have met people over the years who are stuck and unable to grow because they can't make peace with how their lives have unfolded. But if we live yielded to God, He is able to use the trials and hard times to replace coping with character. Character can be formed when we are stretched, strained, and challenged.

"Consider it all joy, my brethren, when you encounter various trials, knowing that the testing of your faith produces endurance. And let endurance have its perfect result, so that you may be perfect and complete, lacking in nothing" (James 1:2–4). James was helping the twelve tribes who became scattered due to persecution to keep hope and perspective. Joy is different from happiness. Happiness is based on circumstances; joy runs much deeper. Warren Wiersbe defined joy as "that inward peace and sufficiency that is not affected by outward circumstances."[11] According to James, the outcome of the endurance formed through trials is being "perfect"—mature and complete.

Paul wrote something similar to the Romans: "Not only this, but we also exult in our tribulations, knowing that tribulation brings about perseverance; and perseverance, proven character; and proven character, hope; and hope does not disappoint, because the love of God has been poured out within our hearts through the Holy Spirit who was given to us" (5:3–5).

Again we see a progression take place from tribulation to perseverance to proven character to hope and ultimately to greater intimacy with God. There are no shortcuts.

In his famous twenty-third psalm, David wrote,

The Lord is my shepherd,
I shall not want.
He makes me lie down in green pastures;
He leads me beside quiet waters.
He restores my soul;
He guides me in the paths of righteousness
For His name's sake.

Even though I walk through the valley of the shadow of death,
I fear no evil, for You are with me;
Your rod and Your staff, they comfort me. (verses 1–4)

Partway through, David switched his description of God from *He* to *You*. *He* makes me lie down, *He* leads, *He* guides . . . but *You* are with me; *Your* rod and *Your* staff comfort me. The *He* becomes *You* in the valley of the shadow of death.

When we endure trials and accept the times when God says no, even when it's a matter of life or death, we end up with an intimacy with Him that cannot be manufactured or taken away, and we are able to trust that He has more for us and those we love than we can see.

This was certainly true when Jesus faced the cross. In the Garden of Gethsemane, Jesus asked His Father if it was possible for Him to escape the suffering and dying on the cross that lay ahead (Matthew 26:39).

God said no.

Even to His beloved Son.

We have the benefit now of looking back two thousand years and seeing God's great plan unfold. God's methods may not make sense to us, but our trust is never misplaced when we surrender our hearts and lives to Him and follow wherever He leads.

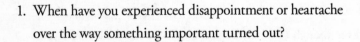 Questions for Reflection and Discussion

1. When have you experienced disappointment or heartache over the way something important turned out?

2. What do you do when you're bewildered about life's events?

3. Have you ever asked God for something and then wished He hadn't said yes? How did the situation play out?

4. Think of a time when God said no. What do you think might be the reason(s)?

5. In retrospect, have you ever been glad God said no? If so, why?

6. Consider the question "Do I welcome only a safe, tame, comfort-granting Jesus, or do I trust Him in *all* His power and majesty?" How do you respond? Why?

7. In what ways has God used your trials to form your character?

8. Are you able to trust that God has more for us and those we love than we can see? If so, on what do you base this faith? If not, what do you think would help you deepen your trust?

8

Embracing Plan B

"My thoughts are not your thoughts, nor are your ways
My ways," declares the LORD. "For as the heavens are
higher than the earth, so are My ways higher than your
ways and My thoughts than your thoughts."

—ISAIAH 55:8–9

Carita and Dennis met at Houston Chinese Church during elementary school and grew up together. She sat in the front row week after week as an eager firstborn nine-year-old, her hand raised enthusiastically, fingers reaching high as she answered all the teacher's questions perfectly. He sat in the back row with all the other rowdy boys. She would turn around in her chair, place her finger to her mouth like a librarian, and sternly say, "Shhhhhh, I'm trying to listen." He just found her annoying.

Both of their large extended families not only attended the church but also faithfully served in leadership roles. Both children were baptized on the same Sunday. And though they attended different high schools, they became friends, then eventually more.

Carita trusted God with her life and followed His lead—willing to go wherever He sent her. She sought to live uprightly, did all the church things, and became heavily involved with campus ministry in college. She became the first full-time vocational missionary sent from the church, and though occasional challenges surfaced, for the most part her life reflected all the best hashtags: #blessed, #lifeisgood, #Godisgood. When she married Dennis, 850 people attended their wedding.

Carita's mom ran a day care of nearly one hundred kids. Carita loved growing up around so many children and looked forward to having her own one day. Dennis came from a large family and also loved being around children. As a dating and young married couple, Dennis and Carita ranked high as favorite babysitters among the families with young kids on their ministry team.

Their first wedding anniversary found them leading a team of college students on a summer mission in East Asia. They celebrated at a nice hotel and happened to see families from the US dining in the same restaurant with their newly adopted children. As they watched the families, both of them agreed they wanted to eventually adopt after they had biological children. Over dinner they planned out when they would begin trying to get pregnant, how far apart their children would be, and how many biological and adopted kids they would have.

After spending the summer in East Asia, they decided to apply to serve there long term. Following their plan in the restaurant, according to their timeline, they began trying to get pregnant. Month after month, nothing happened. A year later they both began to wonder why. None of this made sense. They were young and healthy. They'd both surrendered their lives to follow wherever God would lead. They pursued vocational Christian ministry and gave up other dreams to serve God as full-time missionaries. They wondered and asked God, *Why is this happening to us? We both love children. It's biblical to multiply and have kids.* What was going on? *Is something wrong with us?* they wondered.

Two years of trying led them to see an infertility doctor for testing to find out if underlying medical issues were affecting their ability to get pregnant. They came out with undiagnosed infertility, which meant no clear reason existed why they couldn't have biological children. Carita struggled not only with the inability to conceive but also with feelings of letting Dennis down.

They moved back to the United States and pioneered a new ministry to Asian Americans on the University of Texas campus. They didn't see much fruit during those first years, which matched their own barrenness. Meanwhile more friends married and started families. Attending baby showers became more challenging as conversations turned to nursing babies and birth stories and other experiences Carita didn't share. And though they felt genuine joy for their friends, each announcement seemed as if God was withholding His favor. Most of the other couples their age formed community around their growing families. The loneliness drove them to overfill their days with ministry. Their Asian culture taught them to not talk openly about problems or struggles.

As they underwent doctor's appointments and infertility treatment, Carita began struggling with going on campus at all. Sharing the gospel and telling people "God loves you and has a wonderful plan for your life" felt disingenuous. They had prayed repeatedly that God would give them the desire of their hearts, but with every pregnancy test their hopes were dashed. They exhausted all medical options and their savings. Meanwhile former students they worked with began the having-children stage—the stage they longed for but were barred from.

During this time of bewilderment, Carita found a safe haven, a lifeline of sorts, with other Christian women in an infertility support group. To have her feelings validated, to be assured she wasn't alone or crazy, and to mutually share struggles and the insensitive and hurtful questions and comments of others were a balm for her soul. She didn't carry her pain silently anymore. And from this place of being known and understood, Carita began to experience a newfound freedom. She no longer felt afraid of hearing the question "Why don't you have kids yet?" Now the question became an invitation for those who asked. Carita graciously extended an opportunity for others to know their situation and join their journey by praying with them and for them.

Seven years into their infertility journey, Carita and Dennis decided to move forward with pursuing adoption. They filled out and turned in paperwork for an international adoption from China. They'd heard that domestic adoptions often led to complications, so they didn't pursue that option. They were told that a match from China would take two years.

A year into their wait, they received an email from a friend's adoption attorney inquiring if they would be interested in a domestic adoption. Nothing ever came of the call, but an important connection formed. The following year the same attorney called out of the blue. A birth mom's due date was in one week. A baby boy. Would they be interested?

God's handprints seemed to be all over the situation, which helped them to move forward in faith. They agreed to take the next step to start the paperwork, and the birth mom selected them immediately. For the first time they felt confident to begin preparing for the arrival of their long-awaited baby. They started purchasing and borrowing the baby items they had always wanted. They even picked out a name for their son, something they'd intentionally avoided in the past. They waited with excitement and anticipation for the birth of their child.

The attorney called again a week later to give them the devastating news: the birth mom had changed her mind and wanted someone in her family to take the baby. Was this a cruel joke? Looking around their home at recently acquired baby items and the partially assembled crib that they'd never before dared to purchase, they couldn't even form words.

Too upset to attend church, they stayed home, paralyzed by regret and grief. The phone rang again. This time it was a social worker from the hospital in California, calling to tell them the birth mom had changed her mind again. The social worker informed them of the birth of a healthy boy who was once again available for adoption. They would need to arrive by Tuesday, or social services would place the baby in foster care. The social worker asked if they would be willing to fly out immediately to take custody of the child. In faith, they purchased airline tickets and quickly packed bags, including an infant car seat, with no guarantee that they'd bring the baby home because the legal papers had yet to be signed. Once again, they dared to open their hearts to receive their son.

The church the Chens attended planned on presenting a sermon series on adoption, so those in charge of the series asked Dennis and Carita if a film crew could join them when they flew out to meet their son. Carita had learned to open up and share their journey, not hide their process and their pain. With both humility and generosity, they agreed to allow God to use their story any way He saw fit.

After traveling all day, Dennis, Carita, and the film crew finally arrived at the hospital. When they reached the maternity ward, they were led to a lone baby sleeping in a clear plastic bassinet. With shaky hands Dennis reached for him. Looking down on the child, he choked out the words "Hello, son. I'm your dad, and this is your mom. We've waited so long to finally meet you." That's all he could manage through his tears.

They had waited nine years.

Not What I Thought

All of us experience times when we think, *This isn't how I thought life would go.* As discussed in the previous chapter, if we are willing to walk through grief and accept what will never be, we have the opportunity to surrender and let God lead us along a new path. The longer we live, the more we come to understand: few of us get to live our plan A.

An incident in the New Testament stands out to me as one when Jesus's timing didn't seem to fit the situation. In John 11 we read about Mary and Martha and their brother, Lazarus. This family held a very special place in Jesus's heart. This is the same sibling group we hear about elsewhere in the New Testament who opened their home in

Bethany and hosted Jesus and the disciples. Martha was the frenzied kitchen host—likely the firstborn "responsible" one. Mary was the one sitting at Jesus's feet to soak up His teaching with the other disciples (Luke 10:38–42). Jesus found their home a haven of comfort and safety. In fact, the week before Jesus went to the cross, He chose to spend time with these three in their home, knowing they would minister to Him. Imagine the honor of being selected as people who blessed, encouraged, and filled up the emotional and physical tank of the Son of God before His greatest trial!

So when we read in John 11 that Lazarus became sick, it's hard to understand what happened next. The sisters called for Jesus to come and heal their brother. In their message to Him, they highlighted the family-like relationship they all shared: "Lord, behold, he whom You love is sick" (verse 3). The word *love* in this verse is *phileo* love, which is "brotherly fondness." The love Jesus had for Lazarus came from a place of loyalty, friendship, and deep affection. When Lazarus fell ill, Jesus was in Jerusalem, only two miles from where the siblings lived. But Jesus didn't leave Jerusalem for *two days,* and Lazarus died.

Jesus's response seems cruel. This family sought to honor God and faithfully followed Jesus's teaching. They gave generously of their resources, hosted the disciples, and believed Jesus was the promised Messiah. And yet Jesus didn't save Lazarus. The sisters probably exhausted their options as they sought out doctors and herbal remedies to help their sick brother. They probably watched their brother struggle for breath as his life slipped away and his skin turned cold. As they planned for the burial, they saw reminders of Lazarus everywhere: his empty place at the table, his discarded sandals, his favorite cup. The house felt desolate without his voice and the sound of his footsteps. By the time Jesus arrived, Lazarus had been in the tomb four days. The sisters each said to Jesus, "Lord, if You had been here, my brother would not have died" (verses 21, 32). This smacked of accusation. How could He have let them down so grievously?

In our own times of grief, we join the sisters, wondering, *God, how could You let this happen? It makes no sense.* But in this story we are given a special glimpse into God's heart. He knew what would happen, how He would bring Lazarus back to life and work things out according to His purposes. Yet He fully entered the grief of His friends. He didn't explain it away; He didn't say, "Look on the bright side"; He didn't minimize or dismiss their pain. Rather, He wept. When we suffer, Jesus joins us in our tears and confusion.

In the book of Job, we read of a righteous man whom God allowed Satan to test. Satan took away everything and everyone except Job's wife. Blow after blow Job suffered excruciating pain, both emotionally and physically. In one fell swoop he lost his wealth: his cattle were taken by an enemy army; his servants and sheep were obliterated by fire from heaven; another enemy army took his camels. The loss of his possessions, however, didn't compare to the death of his ten children. This horrendous loss was followed by a physical ailment so severe that his entire body was covered in boils. He sat in ashes and scraped his sores with a piece of broken pottery. Like Martha and Mary, Job felt agonizing grief and confusion.

At the end of the book, God spoke to Job, but He never gave him the backstory or the reason for his suffering. This side of heaven, we may not find out the reasons our lives turned out as they did either. Our choice to live with open hands even when our circumstances don't fit our plans is a decision to have faith in a trustworthy God. Rarely does our choice to surrender in the midst of painful circumstances ever *feel* good. The fact that God did restore Job's fortunes in the end and increase everything twofold, including giving him another seven sons and three daughters, doesn't negate his previous losses. I'm sure he and his wife never stopped missing their first seven sons and three daughters. Each of those children had names, personalities, and gifts. But people are resilient. We manage to make our way through the unspeakable, and most of us come out changed for the better. Our lives are marked by our losses, but we need not be defined by them.

The Bitter and the Sweet

Esther's life, like yours and mine, took unexpected twists and turns. Life did not look the way she imagined as she grew up. Her ambitions didn't include moving to the palace as part of the king's harem, much less living with the pressure of being queen. Her sadness over losing her parents probably never went away. But I imagine that her gratitude for her cousin Mordecai ran deep, and she embraced a role that changed the course of history for the better. Esther held in tension the bitter and the sweet. We, too, must learn to accept both the good and the hard as we walk a path unlike the one we pictured.

Like everyone else, I know the ache of unrealized dreams and disappointments. Back in college I penned the words to this poem:

Waiting Is:
Steadfastness that is holding on;

Patience that is holding back;

Expectancy that is holding the face up;

Obedience that is holding oneself in readiness to go or do;

Listening that is holding quiet and still so as to hear.

The poem joined a mishmash of motivational sayings I collected and carefully copied onto the blank page in the back of my Bible. Many times I would run into Bible study breathless, claiming, "I have a *new* five-year plan!" Little did I know what the future would hold. I had no idea that living open handed and following God's lead would include financial challenges, heartbreaking miscarriages, job and ministry upheaval, food allergies, ADHD, marital strain, years of wilderness wandering as a new mom, therapy, depression, burnout, and, probably most challenging to date, a cancer battle. None of these challenges appeared on any of the eight renditions of my five-year plan. Yet when I look back, I see how each challenge and loss led to a greater understanding of what it means to follow God in a fallen world. Each trial deepened the mystery of God and broadened my understanding of His character; each heartbreak formed a bridge to connecting with others walking similar roads; and each hardship altered my soul as I experienced the generosity and support of a trusted community.

During times of doubt, fear, and uncertainty, we have the opportunity to consider what our belief in God really means in the way we live. Acts 16:31 reads, "Believe in the Lord Jesus, and you will be saved." Mere belief in facts doesn't translate to a life that looks any different from that of someone who does not believe. The question we need to grapple with is, What *kind* of belief do we hold? According to *Vincent's Word Studies,* a sort of combination commentary and Greek lexicon,

> To believe in, or on, is more than mere acceptance of a
> statement. It is so to accept a statement or a person as to rest
> upon them, to trust them practically; to draw upon and avail
> one's self of all that is offered to him in them. Hence to believe
> on the Lord Jesus Christ is not merely to believe the facts of
> His historic life or of His saving energy as facts, but to accept
> Him as Savior, Teacher, Sympathizer, Judge; to rest the soul
> upon Him for present and future salvation, and to accept and
> adopt His precepts and example as binding upon the life.[12]

Life is rarely neat and orderly. Because we exist within the confines of time, we don't see the outcome of each story. More often than not we find ourselves having more questions than answers. God's will, God's ways, and God's timing are wildly unpredictable and rarely what we expect.

One of the greatest challenges we face in living with open hands is being asked to accept life's disappointments and embrace plan B. With willing hearts we choose to wait on God's timing rather than take matters into our own hands. Waiting is not passivity or a detached "Whatever; it doesn't matter." Rather, it is a tough choice to keep our hands open, even when what God asks of us feels painful and unfair. Because we cannot see past the ups and downs and the twists and turns of life, we can't see where our path will lead. We have to wait for more of the story to unfold. And we have to decide for ourselves, *Is God good or not?*

He Is Good

In Dennis and Carita's case, the video of meeting their son went viral.[13] They had no idea how many lives it would touch. As of this writing it has been viewed more than 8.7 million times worldwide! Translated into Chinese, the video aired on the news in Taiwan. Missionaries in China emailed to let the Chens know that their story had been used to share the gospel.

Another friend of the Chens shared how she found her husband crying while on the computer. "You've got to watch this video," he said. She took one look and said to him, "I know them! They were Cru staff at Texas A&M when I was a student. You've even met them at church before!" She asked how he'd come across the video. Her husband is Egyptian and a believer. He said one of his friends in Egypt, who is not a believer, posted it on Facebook. It was then that the Chens realized how God was using their story to spread the good news of the gospel in places where it was not easily shared.

"During our hardest times, I felt abandoned by God," Carita told me. "I felt hopeless. Now, ten years later and after seeing how God has and is continuing to use our adoption story for His glory, we can stand here and say that it has all been worth it. We're not saying the pain isn't real or the anguish of infertility has or will ever completely go away just because we now have what we want—a child. But ultimately it's Jesus who enters our pain and meets our needs."

These words are not trite phrases or opinions but hard-won proclamations of faith and surrender. During our most recent phone conversation, Carita shared with such confidence and grace, "God is 100 percent purposeful in what He does. He hasn't forgotten us."

I've known Carita and Dennis for many years now, and my respect and admiration for them has continued to grow as I've walked, prayed, grieved, and celebrated with them. They have remained authentic and grounded through the darkest times. Their character and maturity shine bright because of their hearts' response during each step of their journey. They motivate me to examine my own life: Do I accept God's will only when it matches my own? Do I equate plan B with absence of love or favor? Do I choose to trust God's character even when my circumstances don't make sense? In the Chronicles of Narnia, Lucy learns about Aslan the Lion, the Christ figure, from the Beavers. She asks whether Aslan is safe. " 'Safe?' said Mr. Beaver . . . 'Who said anything about safe? 'Course he isn't safe. But he's good. He's the King, I tell you.' "[14]

God's ways are not my ways; His thoughts are not my thoughts. I cannot fully grasp all of who God is, but even when His actions or inactions don't make sense to me, I still seek. In the pages of my coffee-stained, tear-stained, well-worn Bible, I catch glimpses of His heart and His mysterious ways. He is good, I tell you. He is a God of redemption and restoration. His purposes cannot be thwarted.

Questions for Reflection and Discussion

1. What did you envision for yourself when you were younger? In what ways are you living your plan A? In what ways are you living plan B?

2. Have you ever felt as if God was withholding His favor in your life or someone else's? If so, how did you handle this, and what did you learn?

3. Think of a time when God's handprints appeared to be all over a situation, yet it didn't turn out the way you expected. How did you respond? Do you think you would respond any differently based on what you know now?

4. Whom do you know who defines herself by her losses? What can you learn from her? Whom do you know who demonstrates faithfulness and trust in God in spite of his trials and disappointments? What can you learn from him?

5. How have you welcomed other people into the disappointing times in your journey? What were the benefits? If you know someone now who could use your support, what might you offer?

6. What are some things you can be grateful for as you live out the plan B parts of your life?

7. As you look back on certain trials, what are some ways God has used them to deepen your experience of Him and change you for the better?

8. Consider the statement "We have to decide for ourselves, *Is God good or not?*" Where are you in regard to this? If you are struggling, ask God to help you see Him more clearly.

9

Serving Without Seeing

You don't have to be blooming to be growing.

—RUTH CHOU SIMONS

During high school my younger sister, Claire, developed an inexplicable burden to pray for the country of Albania. Thanks to a countries-of-the-world shower curtain and Claire's scribbles and circles with a Sharpie pen, I learned that this small country of 2.3 million is nestled next to Greece in southeast Europe. In 1967 the dictator of the country declared Albania "the world's first atheist state."

Claire began to pray earnest, God-sized prayers in and out of the shower. She prayed for doors to open to the gospel. She prayed for the remote villages inaccessible to outsiders. She prayed Albania would one day send Christian missionaries to the Muslim world. From a human perspective these prayers made no sense, as the country remained locked to the outside world, seemingly impenetrable.

Finally, five years after Claire began praying, the communist regime fell, and in 1992 an opportunity opened for my sister to take part in the first Cru summer mission to Albania. Claire applied, raised financial support, got all the necessary immunizations, and with high expectations set out for the country she had circled with a Sharpie and bathed in faith-filled prayer.

She had the worst summer of her life.

The instability of the government led to an economic crisis, which resulted in food shortages. Several nights Claire went to bed hungry, not knowing what food would be accessible the following day. Bouts of illness, swarms of attacking insects, verbal abuse from the Albanian nationals, and all sorts of chaos surrounded my sister throughout the summer.

An Albanian national, Alma, served as a translator while the team worked in the capital city of Tiranë. The team decided to split and cover more ground the second half of their time in the country. Claire, already stretched from the trials she experienced, hoped she would be assigned to the team going to beaches in the nicer northern part of the country, as she had formed a good connection with those team members. Instead, the leadership placed her on the team headed south. Alma would go with Claire and the southern team as they traveled to Vlorë, a spiritually hardened, Muslim-majority part of Albania for the remainder of the summer.

As they headed south, so did Claire's emotions. The mission ended with little to show for all the effort and prayer and expense for the southern team. The spiritual ground was rock hard, and the Albanian nationals didn't appear to be interested in learning about God. The team in the north, however, experienced tremendous openness to the gospel. Claire returned to the US dejected and depressed, and she carried parasites in her intestines.

Obeying Without Seeing

Sometimes God asks us to take steps of faith and trust Him without knowing how our words, actions, and decisions might affect others. Esther found herself in this position after she and her people had fasted for three days in preparation for her to approach the king. Esther was both shrewd and calculating as she invited Xerxes and his minion Haman to two different banquets. Scripture doesn't explain Esther's motives for waiting until the second banquet to petition Xerxes to spare the Jews from Haman's evil plan, but soon we learn how God is always at work behind the scenes.

The king learned that Mordecai had saved his life when he heard, between the two banquets, the report about the assassination plot. Haman had a fit when Xerxes ordered that Mordecai be honored for his loyalty. But that didn't stop Esther from proceeding with her plan. She said to her husband, "If I have found favor in your sight, O king, and if it pleases the king, let my life be given me as my petition, and my people as my request; for we have been sold, I and my people, to be destroyed, to be killed and to be annihilated" (Esther 7:3–4). When the whole truth came out, Haman was the one sentenced to be hanged.

But Esther didn't know this would happen or what the king would do next. She knew him to be moody and fickle, quick to anger, capable of signing off on the destruction of an entire people group without a second thought. She took a big risk without knowing how things would turn out. She had no idea that her cousin Mordecai would end up being promoted to second in command in place of Haman or that the king would give Mordecai a major role in saving the Jews from destruction. Esther simply did what she knew was right, not knowing if she would be successful in persuading the king to spare her people.

My sister, too, got to see for herself that nothing God does is haphazard. Seven years after Claire's miserable summer, Alma, the Albanian translator, was introduced as the first Albanian national staff member at a Cru staff conference. When asked how she began a relationship with Jesus, Alma shared in front of five thousand staff members about the summer of 1992 and how Claire had led her to place her trust in Christ. All those years had gone by with Claire having no idea of the outcome of her service.

Alma and Claire got together at the conference to catch up, and Claire asked about the particulars of how Alma had become a Christian. Alma explained, "Do you remember sitting on the stairs in the dormitory?" Claire nodded. "You asked me a question: 'Alma, are you perfect?' I knew I wasn't perfect. I had spent time the previous summer translating for a different Christian group, but I didn't fully absorb the gospel message. It wasn't until you asked me that question that I understood about being separated from God because of my sin. Everything I had heard about God suddenly fell into place. God used your words to help me begin a relationship with Jesus."

Claire marveled as Alma disclosed all God had done from there. Alma became a spiritual leader in Albania and discipled nearly one hundred women. Albanian nationals joined her staff, and teams showed the *Jesus* film in obscure mountain villages. Albania started sending missionaries to the Muslim world, just as Claire had prayed, first to neighboring Turkey and then beyond. God had turned the officially atheistic country into one in which 96 percent of the people had opportunities to hear the gospel!

That the Lord would allow Claire to hear firsthand about the answers to her shower-curtain prayers is a gift of grace. But many of us don't get to hear the end of the story this side of heaven. More often than not we won't be privy to how our decisions to show up, share our resources, teach the Scriptures, and share our faith result in changed lives.

Picture yourself cutting an apple in half. You can pick out all the seeds and count each and every one. If you take one of those seeds and plant it in the ground, it might grow into a healthy tree, yet you may or may not be around to see it produce apples year after year. Jesus said to His disciples, "Truly, truly, I say to you, unless a grain of wheat falls into the earth and dies, it remains alone; but if it dies, it bears much fruit" (John 12:24). God asks us to take the seeds representing our lives and lay them down for our king. This requires a dying to self and a surrendering to God's will and His unseen purposes. You can count how many seeds are in an apple but not how many apples a seed will produce. We rarely have any idea how much fruit results from the laying down of our lives. We have no control over the outcome of our surrendered lives. What we do control is whether we will choose to live for ourselves or for God.

The God Who Sees

While Mordecai eventually received reward and recognition for his role in saving the king's life, at the time he reported the assassination plot to Queen Esther, he got no monetary compensation, medal or plaque, or even a fruit basket. He happened to be at the right place at the right time. He did the right thing, not for compensation or fanfare.

But still, some token of appreciation would have been appropriate from a king whose life had been spared and who had the means to throw a huge party (Esther 1:4).

It's frustrating enough when we don't see evidence of our actions making a difference in the world, but when all we do isn't even recognized, we can become disheartened. As we try our best to serve God and others, we may do so without being praised or even noticed for our efforts. We pray, have spiritual conversations, show up week after week at the food bank or Sunday school, drive for the car pool, bring meals to neighbors, host the youth group, pay for someone's drink in the drive-through, tutor, write blog posts, sit in meetings, balance ledgers, mop floors, plan events, design websites, style hair, teach calculus, run corporations or nonprofits, or meet with clients suffering unspeakable trauma. The list goes on and on, but our good deeds may go unsung. For some this might not be a big struggle, but for those who are wired to value acknowledgment for their contributions or who thrive on words of affirmation, this state of invisibility may be particularly difficult.

Early in my marriage I remember feeling so lost. The campus ministry I was involved with felt gratifying and purposeful. But after the birth of our son Jonathan, I found myself physically and emotionally depleted. My formerly crazy-zealous "let's do this!" to-do list became frozen in what seemed like a perpetual cryogenic state.

One week Darrin decided to host his UCLA men's Bible study for a dinner at our apartment. I looked forward to having time with the students and catching up on their lives. Visions of imparting deep spiritual truths and offering wise insight on their struggles fueled my meager attempts at straightening up our little home.

With Jonathan happily splashing in the bathtub and his bedtime in sight, I sat on the edge of the tub straining to hear the conversation around the dining room table. Dinner was over, and the conversation sounded lively as everyone dug into the dessert I had made. Suddenly I heard a little voice saying, "Uh-oh. Uh-oh, Mommy."

I looked down and saw the source of the "uh-ohs." My sweet son had the runs in the tub. He was covered, as was the tub and all the bath toys. I managed to clean him off in the sink and put him to bed, then returned to the mess in the bathtub and started cleaning, cleaning, cleaning. As tears of disappointment filled my eyes, I sensed God impress on my heart, *Viv, you think talking about spiritual things with those college students is valuable ministry. But this, this right here—what you are doing now in secret—is equally pleasing to Me. You are participating in valuable ministry. I want you to know that nothing escapes My notice. I see you and I am well pleased.*

When I was finally finished, I entered the dining room to find that the locusts had descended—the food all devoured; the napkins crumpled; Darrin gone to drop off the students so they could study for finals. Once again, I started cleaning, cleaning, cleaning, replaying in my mind the image of the Lord's eyes, full of kindness, watching over me.

In Genesis 16 we see another beautiful example of this in the story of Hagar, a female slave who belonged to Sarah. Most biblical scholars trace Hagar's introduction into the Abraham-Sarah story to an event that occurred four chapters earlier. Genesis 12 recounts a severe famine that led Abraham to journey to Egypt. While there, Abraham lied to the Egyptian pharaoh, telling him Sarah was his sister. Her beauty was so striking that the pharaoh decided to give Abraham sheep, oxen, donkeys, camels, and male and female servants (verse 16) in hopes of winning Abraham's favor. Later God struck the pharaoh and his household with plagues for taking Sarah as his wife. Abraham and his entourage, including Hagar, were escorted out of Egypt.

A decade passed, and childless Sarah began to fret about the future without heirs for Abraham. In that culture women experienced intense pressure to marry and produce sons to carry on the family name. Sarah felt desperate and took matters into her own hands. She ordered Hagar to sleep with Abraham.

Hagar was at the bottom of the barrel, not only as a woman, but also as an Egyptian, a foreigner, an outsider, and a slave. She was considered property without rights and undeserving of payment for her work. When she conceived following her forced union with Sarah's husband, carrying the child of wealthy Abraham gave her status and power for the first time. Hagar responded by treating Sarah with disdain, and Sarah reacted by treating her servant so harshly that Hagar decided to run away. What happened next is extraordinary.

"Now the angel of the LORD found her by a spring of water" (16:7). Worth noting is the use of "the" angel of the LORD rather than "an" angel of the LORD. Most Bible scholars agree that these appearances of the angel of the Lord were theophanies, preincarnate manifestations of the Son of God. A similar appearance took place when Shadrach, Meshach, and Abed-nego were in the fiery furnace. King Nebuchadnezzar looked in and saw the men unbound, walking around with a fourth man who looked like "a son of the gods" (Daniel 3:25).

What's particularly remarkable in Hagar's account is how the angel of the Lord *found* her: He went looking for her and then called her by name. Abraham and Sarah referred to Hagar as "my maid" or "your maid" and never by her name, but here the angel called to her, fully understanding her situation.

An interesting conversation took place between Hagar and the angel. First the angel instructed Hagar to return to Abraham and Sarah. He assured this young Egyptian slave girl that she was going to bear a son and they would both survive. In fact, the angel promised that God would greatly multiply Hagar's descendants so they would be "too many to count" (Genesis 16:10). God even gave the son a name, Ishmael, which means "God hears." Hagar's life mattered and had purpose. God's plan all along included bringing people from every tribe and nation into the family of God.

Then a most extraordinary event took place: Hagar gave *God* a name. She was the only one in all of Scripture to have this honor. She called Him *El Roi,* which translates to "the God who sees me." Hagar, though unseen and unknown because of her standing as a female Egyptian slave, was seen and known by God. Here we see God demonstrating His commitment to valuing and honoring women. He gave Hagar His individual attention even though the child growing in her womb was not the child promised to Abraham in earlier chapters. He affirmed Hagar and granted her a tender encounter, face to face with the God of the universe.

As a woman, a Gentile, and a slave, Hagar easily fell under the title "Least Likely to Have an Extended Conversation with God," yet she did. Her example reminds us how we, too, can draw close to God because He sees us and knows our circumstances. God instructed Hagar to return to Abraham and Sarah because she brought back a truth *they* needed to know and hear: God saw their situation. He hadn't forgotten them.

As we serve without being seen, when no one else notices, God does. He knows every choice we make and every act of service we carry out in His name. Everything we do as we seek to follow His lead matters to Him. We are each part of a grand story. Nothing is insignificant in God's economy. Our lives intersect with others' in perfect precision. He knows. He sees. And He is always at work. God wires and gifts His people for His purposes. All our contributions make it possible for God to move and work as He wills. Each of us plays a vital role.

The apostle Paul wrote to the church in Corinth, "Therefore, my beloved brethren, be steadfast, immovable, always abounding in the work of the Lord, knowing that your toil is not in vain in the Lord" (1 Corinthians 15:58). We can remain steadfast and serve without seeing as we retain an eternal perspective, confident that what we do is never in vain in the eyes of God.

This brings to mind a surprising encounter I had years ago. While I was standing outside Moby Arena on the Colorado State University campus after an evening of inspiring talks for our Cru conference, a woman came running toward me, waving enthusiastically. Out of breath, she stopped and asked, "Are you Vivian? Did you attend the University of Colorado? Did you live in Buckingham Hall?" I nodded as I tried unsuccessfully to place her face and name.

She told me her name and began to explain. "I lived in Buckingham Hall. And I remember on the other wing of the dorm floor where you lived, you led a Bible study every week." I nodded, still not recalling her face. "Well, I remember one week going by every single room asking if anyone had seen the jeans I left in the dorm laundry room. Someone stole them. I popped my head into your room. You were about to start a Bible study, and I asked if anyone had seen my jeans.

No one had, but as I left you called out, 'I'm sorry we didn't see your jeans, but we will pray for you!' The fact that you would pray for me started me on a spiritual journey. I ended up transferring to another school in Virginia the following semester. There I got involved with Cru and became a Christian, and now I'm taking Bible classes this summer. I couldn't wait to see you to say thank you for helping start me on my journey to knowing God."

I had no memory of the lost jeans event. But *wow*. Isn't God incredible? Each of us is a part of a much greater, grander story than we can imagine. God can and does use anyone and can take any situation or circumstance and use it for His purposes, including stolen jeans! God is faithful to redeem and restore, and nothing in His economy is wasted.

I often imagine the day when we will stand face to face with God. I believe we will be completely undone as He reveals how He answered our prayers and brought about His perfect will. One day God will expose all the intricate interweaving of lives—all the prayers, the unexpected conversations, the bumping into just the right person at just the right time, all of it. God's purposes cannot be thwarted.

Having a willing heart means that we obey without seeing the end of the story, entrusting our work and our lives into the hands of the One who sees the end from the beginning (Isaiah 46:10).

Questions for Reflection and Discussion

1. Think of a time when you stepped out in faith even though you weren't sure what the outcome would be. Did you

eventually get to see what God was up to behind the scenes?
If so, describe it.

2. What is your response to the idea that nothing God does is
haphazard? Does this ring true for you? If so, why? If not,
why not?

3. Have you experienced a season in your life when you felt
invisible? If so, what was that like, and how did you
handle it?

4. Think of a time when you did something you felt was good
and right but weren't acknowledged for it. How did you feel
about it, and how did you respond?

5. What are some things you do simply because you want to,
regardless of whether you are noticed or praised?

6. Name at least three things you learned about God in
Hagar's story.

7. Consider this statement: "We are each part of a grand story. Nothing is insignificant in God's economy." How have you experienced this to be true in your life or someone else's?

8. If you could give God a very personal name based on what you've experienced of Him, what would it be?

10

Building Bridges, Not Walls

In times of crisis the wise build bridges, while the foolish build barriers. We must find a way to look after one another as if we were one single tribe.

—T'CHALLA, *Black Panther*

The fifteen-hour time difference between California and Hong Kong meant waking while it was still dark and enduring a predictable afternoon crash. But with only one short week to spend visiting my parents, we determined to squeeze in all we could.

The rocking motion from the ferry ride across the Hong Kong harbor put fifteen-month-old Michael to sleep, but four-year-old Jonathan knelt on a bench and strained his neck to peer out the window as the ferry carried our family across the dark green water. Jonathan watched, eyes barely blinking, as new sights, sounds, smells, and an unfamiliar language filled his naturally inquisitive mind.

The long walkway brimmed with people as we exited the ferry. Jonathan skipped ahead, and then I watched him slow down almost to a stop. He stared at a man who was sitting on a flattened cardboard box, begging. The man had no legs, no teeth, and matted hair, and he was covered with soot and sores. A few coins clanked against the metal canister he tapped on the cement. Scores of people hurried by him acting as if he were invisible.

I watched the wheels turn in Jonathan's head; his young mind had no category for people living in such poverty. I transferred Michael, still fast asleep, into Darrin's arms as something I'd read in Mike Mason's book *The Mystery of Marriage* came to mind: "To be in the presence of even the meanest, lowest, most repulsive specimen of humanity in the world is still to be closer to God than when looking up into a starry sky or at a beautiful sunset."[15]

I pulled Jonathan out of the steady stream of people and knelt down so we could look straight into each other's eyes.

"Buddy, you see the gentleman over there sitting on the cardboard?" He nodded. "I want you to know that this gentleman is made in the image of God. And because he is made in the image of God, he is more beautiful than the sunset. He is precious to God in the same way you and I are."

Every single person on earth has intrinsic dignity and worth because each of us is made in God's image (Genesis 1:27). David described people as fearfully and wonderfully made (Psalm 139:14). Embracing this truth is particularly important during this time when our nation is experiencing increasing tension and division along ethnic, racial, religious, and political lines.

The author of Revelation, the apostle John, described a scene in heaven in which a wide array of people, languages, and cultures all worship the one true God. Revelation 7:9 depicts "a great multitude which no one could count, from every nation and all tribes and peoples and tongues, standing before the throne and before the Lamb." All people and cultures reflect the magnificence of our God. I confess, for a long time whenever I pictured heaven, I envisioned an enormous praise concert with people surrounding a stage, singing worship songs in English. The truth is, heaven will not be one gigantic Hillsong concert, English will not be the only language, and most believers will not be white.

That said, as an ethnically Chinese woman living in the United States, I am treated as a foreigner to this day. Back in elementary school I remember a classmate pulling her eyes back tight and screaming in her high-pitched voice, "Skinny-skinny-flat-nose! Skinny-skinny-flat-nose!" Though I was born in Wisconsin, 100 percent American, I still regularly hear decades later, "Wow, your English is really good. Where are you from?" If I answer, "Colorado," I hear back, "No, where are you *really* from?" To which I answer, "Wisconsin." But I *am* from Colorado. I moved there before I knew how to walk.

I grew up in Boulder with a handful of other Asians and even fewer African Americans, Native Americans, and Latinos. We spoke Chinese in our home, our shoes came off by the front door, and we used chopsticks, ate rice at every meal, and savored dishes like sea cucumber with bamboo shoots. Outside our home we sought to blend into the white-majority culture. With little to no representation of our culture—no Asian dolls, books, community leaders, television or movie characters, magazine models, or role models who looked like me—I just tried my best to fit in.

If you take a grapefruit and cross it with a tangerine, you end up with a tangelo. A tangelo is neither grapefruit nor tangerine but a unique fruit pulling traits from both. This describes my Asian American experience—a blend of Eastern and Western values and perspectives. It's similar to the experience of third culture kids, a term used to describe missionary and other children who grow up overseas, not fitting in either in home country or in host country. I have felt out of place in America as a woman of color, but I haven't felt at home in any of the Asian countries I've visited either. In Asia I might look physically similar to those around me, but I think and dream in English, and my values have been shaped and formed very differently than Asians from Asia.

Another picture flashes in my mind's eye. I was in first grade during our school Halloween parade, standing by the classroom door. As I lined up with my classmates, my straight, waist-length jet-black hair and almond-shaped eyes looked out of place behind my plastic Cinderella princess mask. The costume represented so much of what I couldn't articulate at the time. My true self remained hidden behind a mask, and try as I might, I would never be a white Disney princess.

The Future Is Here

The landscape of America is changing in dramatic ways. The kindergarten class of 2015 was composed of 50 percent ethnic-minority children. These numbers are driven by birth rate, not by immigration. By 2042 the minority population in this country will surpass 50 percent; a white majority will no longer exist. As couples of different ethnicities continue to marry and have kids, our country will become more and more multiracial and multicultural. However, the 2013 American Values Survey indicates that 91 percent of Caucasians have only Caucasian friends.[16]

My kids are mixed race and represent the future of an increasingly diverse America. The last name Mabuni often causes people confusion. Some expect to see an African or Filipino face when they meet one of us. East Indian is the most recent guess I heard. Actually, the island of Okinawa, Japan, is where the name Mabuni originates. Darrin is half Okinawan Japanese, a quarter Portuguese, and a quarter Hawaiian. Yes, he is handsome! This combo, along with my Chinese ethnicity, means that my kids all look completely different from one another. They all have Asian features, but my son Michael pulled the most Portuguese with his fair skin and brown wavy hair.

Around the dinner table the kids share similar stories of experiences they've had with people trying to figure out their ethnic background. Sometimes the ignorance makes us shake our heads in disbelief, such as the comment a white high school classmate recently made to my daughter explaining how Julia was not American, like her, but Asian, even though they were both born in Southern California! Others wonder if they are Chinese, since they look Asian. The conversation goes something like this:

"So you're Chinese?"

"Well, only half, but . . ."

"Oh, then you're Japanese!"

"Well, not exactly. See . . ." And then they try to explain where Okinawa fits into the chain of islands that compose the country of Japan.

When they add in their Native Hawaiian heritage, they are often asked, "Isn't that just the name of citizens of the state?"

"Well, there was this kingdom of people who existed beforehand . . ."

"But, like, how are you part white?"

"Well, there were these explorers . . ." they begin, telling how the Portuguese sailed from Europe to the Hawaiian Islands.

"So what languages do you speak?"

"Other than English? Spanish, so . . ."

You get the picture! Our backgrounds shape who we are and how we relate to the world.

Growing up mixed race has unique challenges. My son Jonathan shared some of his reflections on Facebook:

> There's a sense of being an impostor, in which identifying with a specific part of me feels disingenuous. "I'm not _____ enough." And yet, all of these ethnicities are inextricably linked to me. They've all played a role, small or large, in my upbringing and in how I see and experience things. So if I can't disconnect myself from any of them nor fully embrace each individually, where does that leave me?
>
> We can't just act as if racial differences don't exist. For me, knowing that my ultimate identity lies in being an image bearer of my Creator means that I can celebrate all parts of me. More and more, I see who I am as a gift rather than a burden. I'm still figuring out what it means to interact with the world in light of all of this, but I'm realizing that I don't have to choose between these different aspects of myself, but instead can live at the intersection of all of them.

Facing issues of diversity head-on is part of the reality of my kids' day-to-day lives. They are fortunate in that most of their experiences have been more comical and puzzling than hurtful and offensive.

Think about your own Instagram feed or the contacts in your phone. Are your friend groups diverse? When I think about ethnically diverse friendships, I'm not referring to having a token ethnic friend—"Here's my one Native American friend." Meaningful relationships are forged from sharing meals around a table, visiting each other's homes, investing time in sharing stories, and disclosing struggles and insecurities. If our personal relationships lack diversity—whether it be racial, socioeconomic, generational, or otherwise—then our perception of people different from ourselves will come through media and entertainment. And just to give you an idea of how people of color feel about inaccuracy in media representation, think about your embarrassment and disappointment in the portrayals of Christians in entertainment and media. Ew, right? Yes, the same kinds of feelings are shared by many others when it comes to stereotypes and how we are portrayed in the media.

Over the past several years, I have sat heartbroken, watching in disbelief story after story of discord and injustice taking place all over our country. The advent of social media gives everyone the ability to witness what people of color have sought to explain about their experience all along. The sad and horrific parts of our nation's history are still alive and well. Racism is alive and well. I am not referring solely to individual racist acts. The vast majority of my white sisters do not engage in using racial slurs or march around wearing white KKK hoods, so they don't think the conversation about racism is pertinent to them. But what I'm referring to is a structure of racism that normalizes the white experience as the superior narrative. A good litmus test would be to ask, "How would I truly feel if my child married someone of a different ethnicity? Would I try to talk her out of the decision? What would I say to friends and family about her spouse?"

As the church we have an opportunity to be part of addressing the core issues that keep us divided along racial, ethnic, socioeconomic, political, and religious lines. The challenge is whether we will choose to ignore or engage. The decision to participate in the difficult work of addressing injustice is grueling but deeply rewarding.

In his *New York Times* best-selling book, *Just Mercy* (my personal most-recommended book over the past few years), Bryan Stevenson wrote about his first meeting with Rosa Parks. When Ms. Parks asked about Stevenson's work, he explained the things he does with the Equal Justice Initiative: helping people on death row, freeing people who have been wrongly convicted, ending unfair sentences in criminal cases, helping the poor receive access to legal help, stopping children from being placed in adult jails and prisons, addressing poverty, and educating people on racial history and the need for racial justice, just to name a few. Ms. Parks responded to Stevenson's long list with a smile. "Ooooooh, honey, all that's going to make you tired, tired, tired." After they laughed, she put her finger to his face and spoke to him in a grandmotherly voice. "That's why you've got to be brave, brave, brave."[17]

Loving Our Neighbor

I have often been challenged to evaluate my view of other people: Do I honor those who have different ethnicities or backgrounds? Do I show partiality and favor to those who have status or come from a similar or higher income bracket? Am I willing to extend God's love to those who are not like me, who hold different beliefs?

Part of having a heart willing to bend to God's will is stepping up to address differences and injustices, understanding that we are responding to God's image bearers. This isn't a political issue; it's a *gospel* issue Jesus taught about regularly. As Christians we are called to the ministry of reconciliation (2 Corinthians 5:18–20). We are meant to help people be reconciled to God, and we are commanded to love our neighbor as ourselves.

Jesus told the story of the good Samaritan in Luke 10:29–37 to illustrate the value He places on accepting and loving the people we are most inclined to judge and reject. Here's a quick background of the Samaritans' history from the Old Testament: After David the shepherd boy became king, he started building a magnificent kingdom. Then his son Solomon built on the existing kingdom, making it even more influential. As the family drama unfolded, the kingdom ended up splitting into the northern kingdom of Israel and the southern kingdom of Judah. The capital of the northern kingdom was the city of Samaria, and over time the whole region became known as Samaria.

As mentioned earlier, the northern kingdom was ruled by nineteen consecutive wicked kings who disobeyed God, so God brought judgment on the kingdom and sent the Assyrians to attack. After the Assyrians defeated Israel, some of the Jews remained and married Assyrian settlers, which violated God's law. Their children, the Samaritans, were hated half breeds—unclean according to the Jews. The Jews who returned from exile despised the Samaritans, and this hostility reigned for centuries between the two groups of people.

Jesus shocked His listeners when He placed the Samaritan man as the hero of the story. The man who had been attacked by thieves and left for dead on the road was judged and avoided by the priest and the Levite, the so-called religious people. In contrast, the culturally hated Samaritan acted with generosity and love. Jesus described the Samaritan as the one who felt compassion (verse 33), bandaged up the man's wounds, put him on his own donkey, and brought him to shelter, where he personally took care of him (verse 34). The next day the Samaritan left the man in the care of the innkeeper, giving him the equivalent of two days' wages to cover any extra costs. He told the innkeeper that if more was spent, he would reimburse him when he returned (verse 35). The religious leader who had asked Jesus "Who is my neighbor?" was confounded by this radical example.

John wrote, "Little children, let us not love with word or with tongue, but in deed and truth" (1 John 3:18). If our hearts are surrendered, we will demonstrate God's extravagant love toward others—especially those who are different from us.

Breaking Down Barriers

How do we keep our hearts and hands open during a time in history when our division is so glaring? All around the world we hear of increasing tension and conflict between people groups. It is particularly discouraging to find the church often silent in the midst of injustice. So often we don't know how to best engage, so we instead avoid these issues altogether.

Jesus addressed the Jews' prejudice head-on and challenged those who declared themselves followers of God to love everyone, including those they might normally despise. The apostle Paul faced similar issues regarding the hostility between Jews and Gentiles in the first century. When we read Ephesians 2, we usually focus on the popular verses that explain the gospel: "By grace you have been saved through faith; and that not of yourselves, it is the gift of God; not as a result of works, so that no one may boast. For we are His workmanship, created in Christ Jesus for good works, which God prepared beforehand so that we would walk in them" (verses 8–10). We neglect to read the second half of the chapter, which describes believers as being one in Christ. Jesus broke down the dividing wall of hostility between the Gentiles and the Jews (verse 14).

As the church today we live in a time of increasing division. We have an unprecedented opportunity to address the issues that keep us from loving our neighbors and being united in Christ. I can't help but think of the families, women, and children who seek asylum at our borders. I'm not speaking of undocumented immigrants; I believe we need to address immigration reform and expose policies that are outdated, ill informed, and outright racist. I also believe we are called as Christ's followers to care for refugees who are fleeing their countries because of war, violence, and oppression. "If anyone has the world's goods and sees his brother in need, yet closes his heart against him, how does God's love abide in him?" (1 John 3:17, ESV).

My friend Jenny Yang, senior vice president of advocacy and policy at World Relief, said, "National security and comfort are the new prosperity gospel. We've elevated both at the expense of getting to know our neighbors whom God has called us into relationship with."[18] Jenny works with members of Congress and the presidential administration to improve refugee and immigration policy. She is quick to point out how the current international circumstances may be the answer to years of prayer for revival. God very well may be bringing the world to our doorstep, especially from countries that historically have been closed to the gospel.

Over and over Scripture refers to God's heart for *all* people. In Genesis 12 when God made a covenant with Abraham, His plan for restoration included *everyone*. "In you *all* the families of the earth will be blessed" (verse 3, emphasis mine). After King Xerxes's counterdecree was sent out to protect the Jews, many Gentiles converted: "In each and every province and in each and every city, wherever the king's commandment and his decree arrived, there was gladness and joy for the Jews, a feast and a holiday. And many among the peoples of the land became Jews, for the dread of the Jews had fallen on them" (Esther 8:17).

Jesus prayed that His people would be one (John 17:21), and after His resurrection He gave clear instructions to the disciples to spread the gospel from Jerusalem, to Judea and Samaria, and even to the remotest part of the earth (Acts 1:8). In Matthew 28:19–20, known as the Great Commission, Jesus commanded His followers to make disciples of all the nations, which means all ethnic groups. From the beginning God's plan and purposes included *all* people everywhere.

Opening Our Hearts

Since God created all people and desires for all to know Him, and since loving God and loving neighbor go hand in hand, how, then, do we take intentional steps to open our hearts and lives to image bearers from different backgrounds and belief systems? Sometimes our cultural blinders prevent us from seeing how our structures, systems, and decisions inadvertently exclude people from participating.

My friend Matt shared an inspiring story of a women's Bible study. They met weekly on Wednesdays at 10:00 a.m., as many women's groups across the country tend to do. This predominantly white church bordered a Latino neighborhood, so the leadership team decided to be intentional about being a resource to the community and invited the women in the neighborhood to the Bible study. They asked the obvious first question: "Would you like to check out our women's Bible study?" No one came.

Many people would stop there and might conclude several things:

○ We did our part.

○ They didn't respond.

○ Latinas aren't interested in studying the Bible.

○ They are not serious about growing in their faith, as we are.

Instead, this group of church women had the wisdom to go back and ask the neighborhood Latinas a second question: "Would you help us understand why no one came to the Bible study?" They learned that the women, though interested, had a roadblock. All of them worked weekdays at 10:00 a.m. After their kids went to school, they all went to work.

The church women wisely followed up with a third question: "If you're interested in being in a Bible study with us, what time would work for you?" The women responded with a time when all of them could attend: 10:00 p.m. So the leadership team decided to meet at an hour that was unconventional for them but honored their neighbors' needs. As a result of the time adjustment, the church flooded with women who more accurately reflected the ethnic diversity of the community, and a deep sisterhood of mutual respect formed.

This example of the choices my white sisters made breathes encouragement into me. It underscores practical ways we can open our hands and welcome people who are different from us so that all can participate.

Be the Bridge is an organization founded by my friend Latasha Morrison. The mission of this nationwide nonprofit is to inspire the church to have a distinctive and transformative response to racial division and to be intentional in its efforts toward racial reconciliation. Her organization has developed materials to help train both individuals and organizations to engage in educational and meaningful conversation. I highly recommend checking out her materials, including Whiteness 101.[19]

A note for my sisters of lighter hues: take time to learn about your own cultural and ethnic backgrounds. Two of my closest friends have wonderful ties to their roots. My friend Lisa is from a Dutch American background. We often talk about the similarities in Chinese and Dutch culture. My friend Debbie grew up loving and celebrating her Portuguese heritage. Knowing our roots helps us understand how we have been shaped and the values we carry.

I also recommend expanding your Twitter feed to include voices of color. Continue to educate yourself on history. Learn about the Native American story and the Native Hawaiian story. Read about the Chinese Exclusion Act and the Japanese internment. Watch documentaries on the history of slavery.

In addition to widening our circles to include those from different races and ethnicities, we need to open our minds to views that are different from ours. This doesn't mean we have to adopt them as our own, but if we don't make an effort to understand those with other views on theology and politics, then how can we love these people as our neighbors?

One way to educate ourselves about what people with different views really think is to expand the places from which we take in news. If you watch only the station and read only the publications that reflect your views, consider learning from other sources as well. Many of the debated passages of Scripture have been scrutinized from every imaginable viewpoint over the centuries. We are not the first ones to struggle with differences. Our propensity to tie our identity to our theological views or political views rather than to the Lord may leave us critical, arrogant, judgmental, and ultimately nothing like the God we seek to serve. We would do well to evaluate the narratives to which we subscribe and the sources of our information.

Most important, we need to take time to humbly learn from others. Central to all aspects of building bridges instead of walls is valuing others through genuine listening. Too often we react or respond with self-protection and dismissiveness. Defensive people cannot empathize, much less connect. We cannot create lasting change without first understanding and addressing the root issues that drive our prejudices. The change begins inside each of us.

The topic of diversity is emotionally charged. The issues will only escalate as time goes on. We can be part of the solution by investing time in learning and growing in our awareness. When we intentionally stand up to prejudice and exclusion in its many forms, we can make our world closer to what God had in mind when He created us different from each other.

Questions for Reflection and Discussion

1. What is most likely to come between you and others: race, ethnicity, socioeconomic status, religion, or politics? Why?

2. How do you feel about an increasingly diverse America in which Caucasians will eventually become the minority?

3. If you are not Caucasian, what is the most difficult part of living in America and in your circles in particular? If you are not a person of color, what have you observed about the divisions affecting our society?

4. Do you invite people of different races and ethnicities into your circle? Do you have any close friends who are in one of these categories? If not, what are some specific steps you could take to change this?

5. How do you feel about the current political climate in America and in other parts of the world? What are some ways you might contribute to solutions to the injustices and divisiveness that are so often present?

6. Have you been guilty of religious snobbery? How has this looked? What will you do about it?

7. Whom do you consider your neighbors in the way Jesus referenced them? What prevents you from loving them well?

8. What specific steps can you take to open your heart and life to image bearers from different backgrounds and belief systems?

11

Abiding in the Vine

I am the vine, you are the branches; he who abides in
Me and I in him, he bears much fruit, for apart from
Me you can do nothing.

—JOHN 15:5

Our next-door neighbor hails from Italy. Our kids call him Papa
John, just as his grandkids do. He loves his pasta and makes
homemade pasta sauce with his secret recipe. His round belly confirms
his mastery of the craft. As his neighbors we, too, have enjoyed his
authentic Italian sauce carried over to us in gallon-sized baggies over
the years.

John, like all good Italians, also knows the ins and outs of grape
growing and vineyards. He has, on occasion, brought over to us in a
jelly jar the delicious end product of his harvest.

Grapevines grow along the fence in our backyard too. We enjoyed
a bumper crop of grapes after one especially rainy season. Darrin and

my sons brought the harvest into our kitchen, bowl after bowl of huge grapes. I felt like a pioneer woman of old eating off the land!

A few months later as the weather cooled down, Papa John came over. I watched out the kitchen window as John, with toothpick in his mouth and big, expressive Italian gestures, pointed here, then pointed there, and proceeded to show Darrin how to prune the grapevines. White grapes are pruned one way, red and purple grapes another. Darrin is skilled in so many areas, and whatever he doesn't know he is willing to learn via YouTube. He probably already knew about the different kinds of pruning, but he patiently listened to John explain. John reminds Darrin of his dad, and he misses his dad and the rest of his family living so far away in Hawaii.

Darrin brought out the large vine-hacking tool thing. (I have no idea the proper name for tools—or anything sports related, though I tend to use sports analogies liberally and often incorrectly.) Together the two men started pruning away thick branches full of healthy leaves—the very same branches that had produced those bountiful grapes. As I watched several feet of perfectly robust branches fall to the ground, the Chinese in me exclaimed, *"Ai-ya!"* I could understand the value in cutting away the dry, dead branches, but the ones they removed thrived and flourished and yielded abundant fruit! Pruning seemed so counterintuitive. But sure enough, the next summer the branches grew back stronger and fuller, and the grapes tasted sweeter. I learned a powerful lesson: what for a season may seem like death will actually produce a greater yield in God's time. And just like Papa John, our Father knows how and when to prune our branches to bring us closer to Him and produce the fruit of His Spirit in our lives. The purpose behind the pruning is always so the branches will bear more fruit, and bearing fruit—*much* fruit—glorifies God (John 15:8).

Sometimes we get the wrong idea and think living fruitful lives is prideful; we mistake the meaning of humility, thinking it means we should hold back and live understated. However, as you've perhaps heard before, humility is not thinking less of yourself; it's thinking of yourself less. Jesus taught in His Sermon on the Mount, "Let your light shine before men in such a way that they may see your good works, and glorify your Father who is in heaven" (Matthew 5:16). Our lives and the outcome of our good works bring glory to God, so we should not hold back being who we are and shining brightly for Him and for His purposes.

The True Vine

John 15 is among my top five favorite chapters in the Bible. Jesus's last words to His closest disciples are packed with significance and instruction and give us insight into the priorities of being His followers. Consider how many times the word *love* shows up in chapters 14–17 or how often Jesus referred to prayer and the Holy Spirit. These are the things closest to Jesus's heart and the lessons He wanted to drive home to His disciples during the final meal they shared together.

Jesus began, "I am the true vine, and My Father is the vinedresser" (verse 1). The Vine is the sole source of spiritual nutrients and abundant life. Life is not found in what we often think it is: productivity, material goods, education, leadership positions, family, a meaningful career, Christian morals, or even ministry work. *Jesus alone* is life. In fact, knowing Him is eternal life (17:3).

Jesus used the word *abide* ten times in John 15:4–10. The idea of abiding—or remaining, as some translations use—is having close, intimate contact. Ultimately our focus, rather than on producing fruit, should be on establishing and expanding our connection with Jesus. We have the incredible privilege of unending access to fellowship with God. The writer of Hebrews explained, "Let us draw near with confidence to the throne of grace, so that we may receive mercy and find grace to help in time of need" (4:16). Drawing near does not require a freshly washed face and tucked-in shirt. We come into His presence fully accepted and loved. As children of the Most High, we find mercy and grace in abundance in our time of need, and we are welcomed with open arms.

Now I want to take us a step further. We often think about the Christian life as Jesus *in us,* but this is mentioned only five times in Paul's writings. However, he tells us in 164 places that we are to be *in Christ.* As you read through the New Testament, notice what is true of us *in Christ.* We are made alive in Christ, justified in Christ, sanctified in Christ, seated in the heavenly realms in Christ, and built up in Christ, just to name a few.

By flipping our focus to abiding *in Christ* rather than Jesus *in us,* we position ourselves to participate in the far greater work God is doing all around the world. As we are joined to the Vine and to all others who are also in Christ, we take part in the community aspect of "Your kingdom come, your will be done, on earth as it is in heaven" (Matthew 6:10, esv).

Jesus's commandment to love the Lord your God with all your heart, soul, strength, and mind and love your neighbor as yourself is even more meaningful when we think of doing so in community. The

Eastern culture of Bible times emphasized community. The popular verse found on graduation mugs and sheet cakes reads, "'I know the plans that I have for you,' declares the LORD, 'plans for welfare and not for calamity to give you a future and a hope'" (Jeremiah 29:11). In Western Christianity we have taken this verse to be a promise for our individual lives. The "you" in the original Hebrew language, however, is plural—the Old Testament version of modern-day "all y'all." We are meant to abide in the Vine *together*.

The African proverb proves true over and over: If you want to go fast, go alone. If you want to go far, go together.

Nothing Hurries Time

Abiding in the Vine is paramount, but lately I have been contemplating how nothing can substitute for the *time* element when it comes to bearing fruit. Young grapevines cannot produce the same quality and quantity of grapes that established vines do. Psalm 1:1–3 reads,

> How blessed is the man who does not walk in the counsel
>   of the wicked,
> Nor stand in the path of sinners,
> Nor sit in the seat of scoffers!
> But his delight is in the law of the LORD,
> And in His law he meditates day and night.
> He will be like a tree firmly planted by streams of water,
> Which yields its fruit in its season
> And its leaf does not wither;
> And in whatever he does, he prospers.

Growing an established vine or tree takes time. The psalmist described the tree as "firmly planted by streams of water, which yields its fruit in its season." Young trees do not have enough strength in the branches to bear the weight of a lot of fruit. The establishment of a strong root system and enough girth in the branches is the only way the tree will flourish in the long haul.

In our day we prize youthfulness, as seen through the use of hair coloring, antiwrinkle creams, and the like. We expect immediate results, as we complain and repeatedly hit refresh when a web page fails to load within seconds. We need, more than ever, to recognize the valuable contributions of those who have remained faithful over long spans of time. The perspective of those older and wiser is underappreciated and often overlooked. I have benefited greatly from drawing near to those established "trees" and listening closely to their stories of how they overcame obstacles, triumphed in the midst of disappointment, and learned lessons they carry with them every day.

Betty is one such role model to me. Several months ago I sat at a large round table at the back of the room waiting for a women's Bible study to begin. Betty was the first to arrive. Her smile matched her colorful outfit. She looked right into my eyes and greeted me warmly, and then she looked at my necklace and asked, "Rwanda?"

I nodded enthusiastically. "I went last summer! Have you been?"

She grinned and said, "Several times." Sixty-seven years young, Betty exuded wisdom, grace, and depth every time she participated in our group discussions over the months we met. When I finally heard her story, I learned the source of her intimacy with Jesus.

Raised in a religious cult, Betty knew only a life of striving. The cult adhered to a legalistic, works-based religion with strict rules designed to earn favor and forgiveness from a never-satisfied God. Betty eventually married a man in the cult who turned out to be abusive, just as her father was. When the abuse began to affect her children, Betty decided to run away with her kids and leave the cult.

As a single mom she sought to live life on her own terms. Her daughter, then in her late teens, found a vibrant church and urged Betty to attend. She went to visit because her daughter asked, but she stayed because she truly found the Lord there. For the first time she understood God's great love for her. God the Father was a loving Father, not like the father who had abused her. Betty began to experience deep intimacy with God as their love relationship grew, and she learned to draw spiritual nutrients from the Vine, Jesus.

Betty's strength and fortitude have grown out of numerous painful circumstances in her life. When she married her second husband thirty-two years ago, she didn't know he was keeping a secret. She later learned that he was born in prison to a mother who was an addict and a father who died from a heroin overdose. Raised by his grandma—a streetwise, brothel-running, do-as-I-say-not-as-I-do type of woman who kicked him out of the house every Sunday morning with firm instructions to go to church—her husband learned about a Messiah who loves you where you are. This powerful love encouraged his sobriety until he went to college.

But during college he became an addict himself, and by the time he graduated, he was taking hard-core drugs. Betty tried to take care of him as he battled his addiction for decades. In the midst of that, she lost her firstborn son in a car accident when he was twenty. Almost to the day a year later, her daughter was diagnosed with brain cancer. Fortunately, the surgeons successfully removed a softball-sized tumor, and God gave Betty fifteen additional years with her daughter.

Betty considers the suffering she has been through part of the pruning the Lord has done to bring her to where she is today. As she learned to sink her trust deep into the soil of God's love, strength, and faithfulness, she became one of the most vibrant women I know, and her life is a conduit of blessing to others. Several years ago she took a step of faith by going to Rwanda on a missions trip. She now identifies her greatest passion as accompanying people on their faith journeys. Betty has experienced an abundance of miracles and God's intervention and provision, and she loves being a guide and encouragement to those who want to learn to trust God at ever-deeper levels.

Giving Grapes

In the same way Papa John shares his wisdom and his jelly jars of deliciousness, our fruit is meant to be shared with others rather than hoarded for ourselves. Grapes can be eaten straight off the vine or frozen for half-time soccer snacks. Some have to go through a squashing process as they are made into jellies and jams. Some are made into juices, while some become fine wine. We have a choice about whether to approach life with a mentality of abundance or deficit. What I have found over decades of walking with the Lord is simple: we can never outgive God. Living open handed and sharing our lives and resources are ways to let God use us as a conduit of blessing to a hurting world. We don't really know what the fruit produced in and through our lives will be used for or in what capacity God will use us. Each person's life is unique, and the timeline we are given doesn't look like anyone else's.

My son Michael has always had a tender heart toward God, and his love for God continues to deepen and grow year by year. Even in elementary school he consistently gave whatever he had to God. I remember during my cancer journey how each round of chemotherapy grew more challenging as my body grew weaker. Helping in the lunch line was a privilege reserved for sixth graders. All the sixth graders looked forward to their turn because the helpers were given real pizza from a pizza chain. The week Michael's turn came around, he told me, "Mom, you don't need to make me lunches the next few days. I'm going to fast for you because I think it might help you during this round of chemo." I asked him about serving in the lunch line and the pizza, and he replied, "Yeah, they are having pizza, but this is more important." Michael, as an eleven-year-old, gave what he could to the One he'd learned to trust.

One of the miracles recorded in all four Gospels is the feeding of the five thousand (Matthew 14:13–21; Mark 6:31–44; Luke 9:11–17; John 6:1–14). Huge crowds were following Jesus as He performed miracles, and then Philip, who I imagine had the gift of administration, tried to figure out how much money it would take to feed everyone. Andrew found a little boy who had five barley loaves and two fish, and he brought the lunch to Jesus. Then Jesus took the fish and bread and gave thanks, and the disciples distributed the food. All the people ate until their bellies bulged. As the crowds finished, Jesus told the disciples to gather up the leftovers, and they wound up with twelve basketfuls.

Now, Jesus could easily have made huge mountains of food and formed a buffet line for everyone to walk past, but instead He chose to multiply the lunch over and over and over. It requires faith and trust to believe the food won't run out right before it's our turn to be served.

And as we give away our resources, our lives, our grapes, we need to trust that more will replace what we give. The money, time, people, or resources we need rarely show up in one fell swoop. Rather, we watch as God multiplies over and over, helping to form our hearts to trust *Him* rather than the money or food or grapes.

My friend Sharifa Stevens said, "Jesus takes what little they have, multiples it, and from those meager offerings provides a feast with leftovers. But then, right after this, the disciples get worried because they are sailing but forget to bring bread. That is so much like me. I need to remember to just give the Lord what I have and watch Him multiply it. Afterward, I need to live a life that says, 'I remember, Lord. You did it before and You can do it again.'"[20]

Embracing Messy

When my brother and sister-in-law came to town with their family to drop off their oldest for college, they decided to visit Universal Studios. One of the tours took them to the lot where the outside neighborhood shots for a popular television sitcom were filmed. Afterward, they shared how they'd always admired the pristine, manicured front yards and beautiful flowers on TV. But on the tour, when they looked more closely, they discovered everything was plastic! The entire cul-de-sac looked so real on television, but in reality everything was a facade.

When I look through my Instagram feed, it's easy to forget that the photos don't give the full picture. The beautiful scenic shot I admire doesn't include the humidity and mosquito swarms or the extra hefty mound of droppings left by the moose and bear. Often the cool brick-wall photo is actually located in an alley next to a smelly dumpster. Our Instastories of #livingourbestlife are not real life. The photos are staged and filtered.

The bowls of grapes my husband and sons brought into the house after harvesting them off our vines also contained spiders, ants, dirt, and rotten grapes. The messy part of the grape harvest is simply part of the experience. Life is messy. Complicated. Why does that surprise me? The grapes must be cleaned before they are usable.

Embracing messy is challenging for me because I like to be in control. I like holding the remote control for the TV. I like following the rules and staying safe. Each of us has a different capacity for messy, but for those of us who struggle with control issues, this truth may be particularly difficult to swallow. I've been convicted lately of how often my motive for doing nice things for others is driven by my desire to sidestep anger and disappointment. I do those nice things to manipulate and control rather than to truly love. Sometimes God has to prune me to rid me of my shortcomings.

The Master Gardener is faithful to attend to the weeds that threaten my growth as well. Weeds rob plants of the most vital nutrients in the soil. Some of the ugliest and most relentless weeds growing in our front yard literally wrap themselves around the healthy plants, threatening to choke them out. One observation I've made about weeds is they take *zero* effort to grow. They just do. The weeds by our mailbox grow without any fertilizer or even dirt.

Left untended, my soul gets weedy like our yard, bent toward selfishness and sin. When it comes to removing those weeds, I've found they are easier for God to pull when the ground is damp, and sometimes He uses pain and tears to soften the soil in my soul.

I used to think I landed pretty high on the niceness scale. According to the CliftonStrengths assessment, my top strength is positivity. I'm typically enthusiastic, fun loving, and encouraging. Then I got married. Then I had kids. Then the truth of my selfish and self-protective ways surfaced, and I had nowhere to hide. Nothing has humbled me more than being a wife and mom. Darrin and the kids have seen me at my worst, and I'm sad to admit they have been at the receiving end of my meanest, harshest words and thoughts, as well as my passivity and lack of engagement, which is also rooted in self. Over the years God's Spirit has opened my eyes to my selfish, sinful, controlling ways, and I have needed to humble myself and admit and name the sin. Just like weeds the same sins appear again and again, and I have to apologize repeatedly. Though I don't deserve their grace and love, my husband and kids continue to grant forgiveness.

Some of the severest pruning I have experienced came soon after I hit the milestone when all three of my children attended school all day. New opportunities for ministry opened up for me: I began pursuing a seminary degree, joined a national executive ministry team, and started speaking at more women's events. Life felt fruitful and abundant. Then I received the call no one wants: "You have cancer."

The pruning away of new and meaningful ministry and schooling felt so unfair. I thought I had patiently waited for the right time to engage, and I thought my contributions to kingdom building were useful, helpful, and purposeful. Yet when I look back, I see those years of battling cancer and wandering in the postcancer wilderness as the very things God used to bring about even greater ministry I would not have otherwise known.

Though submitting to the process of pruning requires faith, we can trust the expert hands of the skilled Vinedresser. Though we may not fully understand His ways, His motives are not to harm but to produce in us health and growth. Our Father sees the end from the beginning and knows the right time and the correct season in which to prune us for His good purposes. We would be foolish to compare our pruning process with anyone else's. God is at work in different ways in the lives of all people. No cookie-cutter process exists for becoming more like Jesus. Our yes to His skillful, loving hand in our lives yields untold possibilities.

I've needed to keep these truths front and center. Though pruning and weeding take place for our good, at the time the process *stinks*. But lasting growth and maturity require that the expert hands of the Vinedresser shape us. The blessing of abiding is not so much the fruit and the by-products but the joy of deeper intimacy with Jesus, the Vine. *He* is the blessing.

Questions for Reflection and Discussion

1. Read John 15 in several Bible translations. What stands out to you?

2. Think of a time when you felt that God was pruning you. What was it like, and in what ways are you different as a result?

3. Consider the statement "What for a season may seem like death will actually produce a greater yield in God's time." Name some fruit that grew out of a difficult season in your life.

4. In what ways have your seasons of pruning, growing, and harvesting been messy?

5. Contemplate the difference between having Christ *in you* and being *in Christ.* How does this change the way you think about your relationship with Jesus and with other believers?

6. Think of someone who has faithfully tended her relationship with God over a long period of time. What have you learned from this person?

7. Read Galatians 5:22–23. What specific fruit do you see the Holy Spirit producing in your life? How is God's pruning connected to this harvest?

8. What can you give to others as a result of your bounty? How will you do it?

12

Walking Through Open Doors

A ship in harbor is safe, but that is not what ships are built for.

—JOHN A. SHEDD

As we settled in the living room in a warm patch of sun, I was transported back a quarter century. The same sparkle in her dark brown eyes; the same laugh and dimples; the same hand gestures when emphasizing important points; the same furrow in her brow when she listened to take in new information; the same thoughtful, authentic responses to my questions; the same spunk; the same naturally long, dark lashes. I saw past Danielle's knit cap, which covered a contraption placed under her mostly bald scalp to relieve the buildup of fluid in her brain; the acupuncture needles; her weight loss and weakened body. The breast cancer discovered the previous fall had spread to her brain and lungs, but when I saw the truest part of Danielle, I saw gold.

My earliest recollection of her is meeting her during her freshman year at UCLA through our work with Cru. Danielle managed to bundle all the best qualities into her five-foot-two frame. She was smart, kind, articulate, confident, likable, deeply devoted to God—beautiful inside and out.

Darrin and I had recruited a team made up almost entirely of the UCLA students we worked with, with the intention to go on a summer missions trip to the third-largest unreached megacity in the world. Our departure date was during finals week. Several students arranged to take their finals early. Others faxed in exams from Seattle hours before leaving the country. The dedication and maturity of these student leaders floored me.

Though not recommended, we accepted three freshmen on the team, including Danielle. Most freshmen need more maturing before heading into a potentially stressful international environment, but we felt confident these three would do fine. And they did. When Danielle approached this open door of opportunity, she jumped in with both feet. We lived on the college campus in the foreign student dorms and met local students around campus and in the cafeteria. Along the way God allowed Danielle's path to cross with an East Asian national named Angela. Also a freshman, Angela lived in an extremely cramped dorm room with five others.

As Danielle and Angela spent time together, Angela began to trust and open up about her life. Danielle learned that Angela's father had passed away in the spring, but none of her roommates knew after an entire year of living together. The type of government in this country made trust hard to forge, so Angela remained guarded and careful about disclosing private information, including her grieving heart.

Over time Danielle became Angela's trusted friend, and their conversation often included spiritual topics. Danielle shared about her belief in God, her relationship with Him, and the gift of eternal life through Christ. As they sat together on a bench on campus, Danielle, as a spiritual midwife, witnessed spiritual birth as Angela surrendered her life to Jesus. All around them angels rejoiced. This took place before the introduction of social media and cell phones, so unfortunately the two lost contact at the end of the summer.

Danielle continued to grow and mature as a leader back on the UCLA campus. After graduation God led her through more open doors. She moved to Paris, France, to continue her ministry. This decision made sense, as Danielle grew up speaking French with her father, who was born and raised in Switzerland. The ministry in Paris, however, spread beyond French nationals. Paris drew people from all over the world, including North Africa and the Middle East.

At a Cru function she happened to meet another student from East Asia. As they conversed, Danielle realized this student attended the same university where our team had spent the summer. The student asked more questions and then gasped, "You're Danielle!"

"Yes, I'm Danielle."

"No, I mean you're *Danielle!*"

This student shared that Angela—the same Angela whom Danielle had led to the Lord—had discipled her. Danielle was this student's spiritual grandmother!

None of us forget the people who share with us Jesus's message of life and hope; they become permanently woven into the story of our spiritual journeys. Danielle learned about how Angela had continued to grow in her faith and how the ministry had expanded after our time in East Asia. Angela became the first full-time national Cru staff worker to graduate from her campus. Amazingly, in the middle of Paris, Danielle got to hear how her willingness to walk through doors God opened led to lives being eternally changed.

Some Opportunities Are Scary

During the time of King Xerxes, the seven princes of Persia mentioned in Esther 1:14 advised the king and enjoyed exclusive access to his presence. As mentioned earlier, all others, even royalty, could come to him only if summoned. *Concerned* is too tame a word to describe Esther's state of mind when the time came for her to approach the king in behalf of her people. Probably a better word is *terrified*.

While fasting as an expression of dependence and humility, Esther and all the Jews cried out to God. The specter of certain annihilation loomed. Esther's courageous action to approach the king without being summoned already broke the law. Requesting something of him was unheard of. Yet Esther dared to walk through the door in front of her. I wonder what kind of wrestling she went through the night before she approached the king. Hungry and thirsty from fasting and likely unable to sleep, did she stay up all night? Did her maidens keep her company? Did she experience God's peace and comfort? The text doesn't say, but we do know the result of her willing heart.

Walking through open doors can be risky, and what we encounter on the other side is not always a happy ending like Esther's. We can't imagine a better plan than to live a long, relatively pain-free life and enjoy the blessing of a close-knit family, many dear friends, a meaningful career, and enough money in the bank for a rainy day. But this is not reality for most of us. Like you, I have friends and family walking through dark days of chronic pain, terminal cancer, mental illness, financial setbacks, divorce, prodigal children, aging parents, unemployment, lawsuits, and church splits. Instagram posts don't show the pain of broken engagements, the tears at the end of last night's fight, the notice of eviction, the ultrasound of the baby who no longer has a heartbeat, the news of infidelity, or the challenge of having to start all over after another move. But God is not taken off guard by what we or our loved ones are walking through. He never leaves us, though at times His voice may be difficult to hear. His heart breaks with ours when we walk through a door that leads to a painful or difficult season.

My friend Judy walked through a door into a situation she never planned on or imagined. Judy exudes warmth, kindness, and joy in Christ. Her disposition is gracious, her words are honest, and she lives to glorify God. Her countenance comes directly from her hard-won intimacy with God, forged through difficult circumstances.

In August 2007 Judy's world flipped upside down when her husband, Scott, came home from a doctor's appointment with an explanation for why he was having trouble with his fine motor skills. The diagnosis of the terminal illness—ALS, or Lou Gehrig's disease—sent Judy literally to her knees. Most people diagnosed with ALS die within two years. Scott and Judy had three small children. Kneeling on the cold cement in her garage, Judy pleaded, *God, don't ever leave my side. And when I get lost and can't see You, please make Yourself known to me in an obvious way.* Judy promised the Lord to be as faithful as she could, choosing to trust Him through what she knew would be the most challenging years of her life.

Scott's health continued to decline. Two months after his diagnosis, he came home midway through his workday and got out of the car with his pants around his ankles. He could no longer pull up his pants by himself after using the restroom. When he stopped working, Judy cut back her hours, setting Scott up with what he needed for the day. But by the end of the year, Scott's health had deteriorated to the point of needing around-the-clock care. Each week Scott and Judy grieved as they said goodbye to another physical ability that would never return. Finally, Judy had to stop working so she could devote herself full time to her husband's care.

Micah 6:8 reads, "He has told you, O man, what is good; and what does the LORD require of you but to do justice, to love kindness, and to walk humbly with your God?" Judy clung to the phrase "what does the LORD require of you" whenever she felt exhausted, scared, or overwhelmed. She believed that whatever she faced was exactly what the Lord required; thus, He would provide what she needed because He could be trusted to be faithful. As Judy sought to be faithful to Him, her relationship with Him deepened, and so did her love for Scott.

Greater Love

During Jesus's last meal with His disciples, He said, "Greater love has no one than this, that one lay down his life for his friends" (John 15:13). The word *life* in Greek, the original language of the New Testament, can be translated with three different words: *bios, zoe,* and *psuche.* Bios is the duration of earthly life; zoe is the inextinguishable and indestructible quality of God that He shares with us, making us eternal beings; and psuche is the inner life of a person, equivalent to ego or personality—a person's individual distinctness. In other words, bios is extrinsic life, zoe is intrinsic life, and psuche is the seat of a person's feelings, desires, affections, and aversions.[21]

The Greek word translated as "life" in John 15:13 is *psuche,* calling us to demonstrate greater love by laying down our ego, personality, feelings, desires, and affections. This type of surrender is different from pushing someone out of harm's way and dying in his place. Laying down our physical lives for another (bios) can occur only one time, but laying down our lives day by day (psuche) is dying to ourselves and our wants and ways to show preference and love toward someone else. This kind of surrender can happen over and over. Every day Judy chose to lay down her life. Daily she chose to let go of her hopes and dreams. She took to heart the words she read from her Bible and knew that as she served Scott, she served the Lord.

By January 2008 Judy and Scott were both home and out of work. They entered a time of trusting God in ways they never had before. They had no income and no disability compensation, yet they had a mortgage payment and medical bills exceeding $100,000. They prayed to be able to stay in their home so their kids could have some normalcy. While Judy asked this of the Lord, she remained willing to move if necessary. God delighted in revealing His faithfulness. As they trusted, they watched God provide. They began to allow others into their story and experienced the blessing of community. An unemployed father of five regularly gave them varying amounts of money to help offset their medical bills. People they didn't know showed up with hot meals. Judy would wonder how an electric bill would be paid, and the exact amount, down to the penny, would arrive as a gift. Just as Judy had prayed on the floor of the garage, God was making Himself known in obvious ways.

Scott never complained, and he spoke words Judy held on to:

"Everything we are going through is for someone else; our part is to be faithful." As their trust in God deepened, their extended family began to notice. Before, only their immediate family of five attended church, but little by little their extended family began to show interest. Eventually, twenty-five of their relatives filled an entire section at their church. Scott and Judy watched all their nephews and nieces get baptized. Their relatives' lives changed for eternity.

As mentioned earlier, most people diagnosed with ALS die within two years. God granted Scott more years with his family, and during those years Judy clung to the Lord, who never left her side. For the last three and a half years of Scott's life, a ventilator kept him breathing. He was particularly susceptible to getting pneumonia, so Judy had to suction his lungs anywhere from four times an hour on a good day to every three minutes on a bad one. This meant no sleep for Judy. The character and fortitude she demonstrated through ten years of constant care for Scott set Judy apart as a truly outstanding role model of selflessness. And God faithfully strengthened Judy despite the exhaustion and difficulty. He never left her side.

When Scott lost the ability to speak, he learned to communicate with his eyes. He spent time in and out of the hospital and survived several scares where he coded and should have died. Each time they wound up in the hospital, Judy surrendered and prayed, *Whatever is Your will, I trust You.* She knew a time would come when Scott would have to go, but she wanted more time to say goodbye. The overwhelming peace, the strong sense of God's presence, the outpouring of love through the years of caring for her husband—all these, Judy believes, were God's gifts to her. For Judy, as for Esther, living with open hands meant that her very life belonged to God and rested in His hands.

Judy recorded some of the things she learned during her painful journey after Scott walked into eternity to the Savior he loved and served:

> "He led [them] about" (Deuteronomy 32:10). God led the Israelites "about." He led them around, back and forth, to and fro, round and round, here and there, place to place, in all directions. He led them about, and sometimes He does the same to us. The best way out of our situation or through the trial is not always the fastest way or the shortest way. We don't always like this . . . but yes, God sometimes directs us via the longest route. We may get tired and weary, our spirits may even feel broken from the journey . . . but if we leave the choice to Him, we can trust that His route is the way of deliverance. If we leave the choice to Him, we can find rest in the fact that He doesn't take shortcuts to His best. If we leave the choice to Him, we can be assured that He'll strengthen us to persevere. If we leave the choice to Him, His grace is ours. Long or short, winding or straight, rocky or smooth, by darkness or light, God's way is always best . . . and His best is our best. Hang on . . . keep going . . . and follow Him about.

Hands Cupped Up

In the living room with Danielle, I watched the sunbeams fall gently on her shoulders. She showed me her physical posture of choice: her arms open as if to receive a sleeping baby, her hands cupped upward.

In this place she graciously received the prayers prayed in her behalf. Her hands remained open to receive news from her doctors, including the disappointing setbacks. Her hands were cupped up to receive with humble gratitude the help and love poured out to her and her family. And in this same posture, Danielle worshipped God.

When the doctors discovered the cancerous tumors in her brain, they performed emergency surgery. Radiation followed and required her to have her head screwed into a face mask as she lay flat and had to remain perfectly still for six to seven minutes at a time. The tumors in her lungs made breathing difficult, especially when she lay flat. Her husband, Mynor, posted a black-and-white photo of Danielle's delicate hand in the hospital bed. In her hand she held a smooth, rounded wooden cross, the thick wood grain contrasting light and dark. Mynor's update read, "Danielle completed her five sessions of radiation. She was strong throughout the sessions, praying intently as we were wheeled to and from our room. Her prayer was consistent: 'I trust You, Lord.'"

A life well lived is a life surrendered. The day after we sat together in her living room, Danielle started using oxygen continuously. Two and a half weeks later, she walked through the final door and met Jesus's wide-open embrace in heaven. I picture His huge smile, His words of love and praise.

Here on earth Danielle's presence is deeply missed by all whose lives she touched—the soccer families, the faculty and families at the charter school she helped establish, her church, and her immediate family. She touched thousands of lives. Every seat in her very large church was filled during her memorial service, and people stood along the walls and at the back, evidence of the impact she had in her forty-three years of life on earth.

None of us knows what circumstances we will face during our lifetimes. We are not privy to the challenges or the blessings that await us. What God asks of us is to follow His lead as we seek His will.

Knowing God's will doesn't have to be complicated. As we live with hands cupped up, abiding in the Vine, we don't need to fret about missing God's will or His way. As the ever-wise Jill Briscoe said (in her British accent), "Go where we are sent, stay where we are put, unpack as if we are never going to leave, and give what we've got until we are done."[22]

 Questions for Reflection and Discussion

1. Think of someone you know whose spiritual journey has inspired you. What have you learned from her?

2. Describe a time when you or someone you know had an eternal impact on another person.

3. Think back on a time when an opportunity you were given was particularly scary. Did you walk through the door? What happened, and what did you learn?

4. What door are you being called to walk through now? Are you willing to trust God's faithfulness?

5. Spend some time considering Micah 6:8: "He has told you, O man, what is good; and what does the LORD require of you but to do justice, to love kindness, and to walk humbly with your God?" What does this mean to you at this time?

6. Think of a time when your intimacy with God deepened because you walked through an open door. What did you learn about Him that you hadn't fully internalized before?

7. Contemplate this statement: "Laying down our lives day by day (psuche) is dying to ourselves and our wants and ways to show preference and love toward someone else." How can you practice psuche?

8. In your next time of prayer, consider opening your hands cupped up. Come back to this chapter after a month of practicing this posture of the heart and record your experience.

Final Thoughts

Our travel together is coming to a close. We've covered a lot of ground, exploring what it means to live with open hands and a willing heart. The story of Esther has guided our examination of the posture of our hearts and our discovery of what surrender looks like. We've looked at the unchanging character of God, and we've seen how if we aren't intentional in trusting that character, our tendencies toward apathy, entitlement, self-reliance, busyness, and bitterness can keep us clenching our fists rather than releasing our lives to Him.

None of us knows the doors we will be called to walk through, but at a women's event my friend Kat Armstrong shared a fantastic perspective shifter: our callings are different from our assignments. Our callings never change. They will always be to God, for God, and with God. Our assignments, on the other hand, change as our roles change.[23]

Each of us is on assignment until God calls us home. If we still have breath in our lungs and heartbeats in our chests, rest assured, God has a plan for us. So let us remain faithful to our King as we seek to remain true to our callings. May we walk with integrity and humility, serving even if we can't see the outcome.

When our assignments take us to places of new surrender where we embrace living plan B, enter into the hard work of bridge building, or need to accept a no from God, may we do so connected to the true Vine, and may we rely on Him as our source and focus. May our intimacy with Jesus grow ever deeper. For truly He is the blessing, and living by Him, through Him, and to Him is the most rewarding way of life.

My daughter, Julia, while away at camp, found herself led by God to pray for her fellow campers as she walked the grounds. She would head in one direction, and if her path seemed blocked or if she came to a locked door, she would simply ask, *So now what, Jesus?* And the Lord faithfully guided and redirected her steps. The sweet combination of her willing heart and her awareness of both the presence and leading of her Savior is the picture I leave with you.

May we follow her example and walk closely with the Lord, with open hands and willing hearts, inquiring of Him as we go, *So now what, Jesus?*

The end is really the beginning . . .

Acknowledgments

I'm sitting at my desk right now. I've logged a lot of hours here and gained several pounds. I can't believe the time has come to push send and have the MacBook deliver all these words, which eventually will turn into the book you hold in your hands. Glancing around, I see notes of encouragement from family and friends taped onto the desk lamp, walls, and bookshelves. These words have carried me and kept me company for a full calendar year. My favorite one is from my husband, Darrin: "In case of emergency, open bag and text the ECH (Emergency Coffee Hotline)." Nestled inside the bag I found a custard-filled doughnut. Yes, writing has resulted in a level of anguish so great I had to open the emergency bag . . . and eating doughnuts has contributed to weight gain.

My gratitude runs deep for so many who helped in the process of book writing. Thank you, #IF:Rwanda2017 sisters: Amy, Amber, Emily, Jen, Jenifer, Abby, Jessica P., Jessica Z., Judy, Kendall, Kim, Morgan, Lauren, Lindsey, Margaret, Meagan, Morgan, Nicole, Sissy, Stephanie, and Tanna. You are woven into my heart, and I felt your love and prayers throughout the writing of this book. I cherish the memory of reading the first parts of the unedited manuscript on the balcony of the guesthouse in Kigali. Thank you for lavishing me with a steady stream of prayer, love, gifts, tasty treats, and encouragement during the long, long days of writing.

Thank you, Jennie, for writing the forward to this book and living out open hands and a willing heart in real time. Thank you to the IF:Gathering sisterhood. What a joy and honor to run the race with so many kindred spirits. Thank you, Africa New Life, for the incredible opportunity to meet Rwandan family this side of heaven. May all of us together lift Jesus high.

So grateful for all those who shared parts of their stories: Florence Mugisha, Una Mulale, Sarah Yetter, Tricia Beebee, Maegan McCoy, Carita Chen, Claire Yang, Betty Hopkins, Danielle Montiel, and Judy Steadman. And thank you to those who shared quotes: Jenny Yang, Kat Armstrong, Sharifa Stevens, and Jill Briscoe.

Crossroads Community Church, our home church, thanks for being a stable, safe refuge and home base. Thank you, Dr. John Hutchison, chair of the Department of Bible Exposition and professor at Talbot School of Theology, for taking time to read my Esther summary and answer questions about some of the historical culture surrounding the events of Xerxes's kingdom. Thank you for your words of encouragement regarding my research and papers and words of belief in me to continue my seminary studies. Cru and Epic Movement staff, thanks for serving the Lord wholeheartedly. Thank you to the launch team for sharing the message of this book with excitement, creativity, and heart. Special shout-out to my Asian American and women of color sisters. #representationmatters. May we continue to see more of our faces and voices in these spaces in the coming years.

Appreciation unending for Kenny Wong, photographer, website guru, and expert in all things having to do with design. Traci Mullins, editor extraordinaire—so honored to work with you and learn from you. Truly you are one of the very best! Andrea Heinecke and Alive Literary Agency, thank you for believing in this author and the book and for finding the perfect home. Laura Barker, vice president and editor in chief, thank you for seeking me out over the months and years and listening with genuine interest. I'm so proud and excited to be part of the WaterBrook family. Thank you to the entire WaterBrook team, especially Johanna Inwood, Jamie Lapeyrolerie, and Lisa Beech. Your boundless enthusiasm provided needed guidance and encouragement.

Forever blessed by friendships forged at conferences and maintained over Voxer and shared meals in cities across the country: Amena, Jo, Tasha, and SoCal locals Chantel (Armor Bearer) and Grace. A special thank-you to those who endorsed this book, whom I am honored to call friends. Deep gratitude for Karen Yates and Helen Lee. You remain so kind and generous in sharing perspective, encouragement, and wisdom. Thank you to lifers Leila Wong, Lisa Murtaugh, Margaret Yu, Charmaine Lillestrand, Cynci Petersen, Kelly Sasaki, Lucy Kaneshiro, Debbie Hetschel, and Jamie Lam—you've known me the longest and keep me grounded. So grateful for friends who are family.

Grateful for Hawaii *ohana,* thank you for loving so well and sending so many nephews and nieces our direction! Mom and Dad, unending thank-yous for your sacrifices, example, and generosity. Each year my appreciation for you deepens. And thank you, Claire, for your heart, wit, and faithfulness.

Jonathan, Michael, and Julia, wow, it's been a year of change, challenge, and transition. So proud of each of you—who you are and who you are becoming. Every front-row seat at all your many milestones is an absolute privilege and delight. What joy to watch your lives unfold as you walk with the Lord.

Darrin, at this point we've spent more years together than we have apart. Thank you for not giving up, for loving me at my worst. Thank you for seeing further and consistently prioritizing family and marriage. I feel very undeserving of you and grateful for you. Thank you for all the ways you have loved and served the kids and me.

Finally, thank You, Jesus. You are the blessing. You are good. You are my king. From my very first yes to You when I opened my heart in willingness to follow wherever You would lead, You have proven over and over to be utterly faithful. May this book help people live fully surrendered to You and Your will and Your ways.

Notes

1. Adapted from the book of Esther in the Bible.
2. One helpful resource on this topic is the book *When Helping Hurts: How to Alleviate Poverty Without Hurting the Poor . . . and Yourself* by Steve Corbett and Brian Fikkert (Chicago: Moody, 2012).
3. William Barclay, *New Testament Words* (Louisville, KY: Westminster John Knox, 1964), 242.
4. Sally Breedlove, *Choosing Rest: Cultivating a Sunday Heart in a Monday World* (Colorado Springs, CO: NavPress, 2002), 25–26.
5. Breedlove, *Choosing Rest*, 28.
6. Peter Scazzero, *The Emotionally Healthy Leader: How Transforming Your Inner Life Will Deeply Transform Your Church, Team, and the World* (Grand Rapids, MI: Zondervan, 2015), 14–17.
7. Scazzero, *The Emotionally Healthy Leader*, 147–49.
8. John Ortberg, *Soul Keeping: Caring for the Most Important Part of You* (Grand Rapids, MI: Zondervan, 2014), 14.
9. Corrie ten Boom, *Tramp for the Lord* (Old Tappan, NJ: Revell, 1974), 57.
10. Henry Cloud and John Townsend, *How People Grow: What the Bible Reveals about Personal Growth* (Grand Rapids, MI: Zondervan, 2001), 228.

11. Warren Wiersbe, *Be Free* (Colorado Springs, CO: David C Cook, 1975), 135.

12. Marvin Vincent, "John 1:12," *Vincent's Word Studies,* Bible Hub, https://biblehub.com/commentaries/vws/john/1.htm.

13. "Jacob Chen: An Adoption Story," The Austin Stone, October 22, 2012, YouTube video, 8:56, www.youtube.com /watch?v=ZLOgtobOWHQ&feature=youtu.be.

14. C. S. Lewis, *The Lion, the Witch, and the Wardrobe* (New York: HarperCollins, 1950), 80.

15. Mike Mason, *The Mystery of Marriage: Meditations on the Miracle* (Sisters, OR: Multnomah, 1985), 38.

16. Daniel Cox, Juhem Navarro-Rivera, and Robert P. Jones, "Race, Religion, and Political Affiliation of Americans' Core Social Networks," PRRI, August 3, 2016, www.prri.org /research/poll-race-religion-politics-americans-social-networks/.

17. Bryan Stevenson, *Just Mercy: A Story of Justice and Redemption* (New York: Spiegel & Grau, 2014), 293.

18. Jenny Yang, main stage panel, Catalyst Atlanta 2016, Atlanta, GA, October 6, 2016.

19. Latasha Morrison, founder of Be the Bridge, http: //beabridgebuilder.com.

20. Kay Daigle, "Meet Sharifa Stevens, New BOW Team Member," Beyond Ordinary Women, June 28, 2018, https://beyondordinarywomen.org/meet-sharifa-stevens -new-bow-team-member/.

21. Gary Hill and Gleason L. Archer, *The Discovery Bible: New Testament* (Chicago: Moody, 1985), 537–38.

22. Jill Briscoe, conversation with the author, IF:Lead 2018, Dallas, TX, September 28, 2018. Jill pretty much broke the internet after she shared this idea in her phenomenal, jaw-dropping, conference-favorite talk at IF:Gathering 2017.

23. Kat Armstrong, "Calling Versus Assignment" (lecture, Camp Well, Lost Valley Ranch, Sedalia, CO, October 29, 2017).

About the Author

Vivian Mabuni is a national speaker and writer with a passion to influence college campuses, families, churches, communities, and the world by sharing the hope and life found through intimacy with God. Her first book, *Warrior in Pink,* details how she found a deeper intimacy with God in her journey through cancer as a young mother of three.

With thirty years of ministry experience on staff with Cru, Vivian loves teaching about the Bible and highlighting its practical application to ministry and life. She and Darrin, her husband of more than twenty-seven years, live in Mission Viejo, California, and are parents to Jonathan, Michael, and Julia.

Vivian loves coffee, shoes, sushi, and social media, so stay in touch with her at www.vivianmabuni.com or on Instagram/Twitter: @ vivmabuni.